S0-BDL-146

10 3/98

HALF
PRICE BOOKS

$ 6.48

SERVANTS OF THE BUDDHA

Servants of the Buddha
Winter in a Himalayan Convent

Anna Grimshaw

The Pilgrim Press
Cleveland, Ohio

Originally published by Open Letters, London.
© 1992 by Anna Grimshaw

Pilgrim Press edition published 1994
The Pilgrim Press, Cleveland, Ohio 44115

All rights reserved

Cover design by Martha A. Clark

Printed in the United States of America
The paper used in this publication is acid free

99 98 97 96 95 94   5 4 3 2 1

Library of Congress Cataloging-in-Publication Data

Grimshaw, Anna.
   Servants of the Buddha : winter in a Himalayan convent / Anna Grimshaw.
— Pilgrim Press ed.
          p.   cm.
   Originally published: London : Open Letters, 1992.
   ISBN 0-8298-0963-5 (alk paper)
   1. Grimshaw, Anna.   2. Monastic and religious life (Buddhism)—India
—Ladhāk. 3. Rizong (Monastery : Ladhāk, India) 4. Monastic and religious life
of women. I. Title.
BQ960.R35A3   1994
294.3'657'09546—dc20   93-34019
                                             CIP

For the women of Julichang

Contents

Acknowledgments ix

Prologue 1

Part One: Autumn 3

Part Two: The Coming of Winter 37

Part Three: New Year 73

Part Four: The Storm and After 113

Index 154

Acknowledgments

Servants of the Buddha is based upon my life with a community of women in the Himalayas. It is the imaginative re-creation of an experience that took place more than a decade ago.

In the writing of this book, I have been greatly assisted by Loulou Brown, Peter Fryer, Keith Hart, Norma Meacock, Jim Murray and Louise Simpson. The inspiration for the memoir, however, came from my association with Edmund Leach and C. L. R. James. Sadly, neither lived to see its completion.

Finally, I would like to thank Ros de Lanerolle for her commitment to the publication of this book.

Prologue

I hoisted the empty straw basket on to my back and set off for the monastery. I walked slowly along the sandy path which ran at the side of the river. For almost four months now the river had been silent. At the beginning of the long, harsh winter it had frozen over with a thick crust of ice; but I knew that beneath the surface the water was still dangerously fast flowing.

The day before I had returned from the woods with the nunnery's herd of cattle. One cow was missing, and it was feared that it might have strayed on to the ice, slipped and become stranded with a broken leg. When the animal did not appear the next day, three of the nuns from Julichang went in search of it. Eventually they found the cow. It was barely alive, lying partially submerged in the freezing water of the river. Clumps of ice hung from the animal's coat, weighing it down and making it very difficult for the women to manoeuvre it on to the bank. Drawing on their combined physical strength, they had finally succeeded in heaving the cow out of the river and on to the land. I met them as they struggled to drag the numbed, frightened animal back to the nunnery courtyard. The women stopped, seeking to catch their breath and, with much hilarity, we joked about my hopeless and clumsy attempt to learn spinning earlier that morning.

I left them and continued on my way, following the steep winding track which led to Rizong. I knew it well, for every day, in the late afternoon, I went to the monastery to collect supplies for the nuns (spices, tea, salt, and flour) and to bring the cattle back to Julichang for evening milking. I began to climb higher, beyond the dark narrow valley which housed the nunnery and which had shut out the sun for over a month. The altitude began to sap my strength. Breathless, I paused once I reached the warm sunshine bathing the upper slopes of the mountainside. I took off my heavy boots and propped myself up against a pile of stones. Here I planned to rest until I had shaken off the chill from my morning's work with the nuns.

Usually it was a precious time. I was alone and temporarily relieved from the strains of living in another language and culture. But today I couldn't rest. I had an uneasy feeling. Something bothered me, but I couldn't quite identify what it was. I kept thinking about the arrival of a group of Indian men at the nunnery the day before. On seeing them I had felt nervous and had gone into the kitchen to be out of their sight. This incident kept running through my head, even though I tried to reassure myself that there was nothing sinister about it.

Suddenly three policemen came round the bend in the path. In an instant I knew they were looking for me. One of them called out in Ladakhi, asking if the path led to the monastery and if I had seen a young Englishwoman pass this way. From a distance, the policemen at first mistook me for a local woman; I was, after all, heavily clad in Ladakhi robes and dark from months of barely washing. As they came closer, however, they realized that they had come across the very person they were looking for. They were prepared. Two of the men were armed, and a third stepped forward to hand me an official paper. It was an order from the Ministry of Defence demanding my immediate apprehension.

My life with the nuns of Julichang came to an abrupt end and I was plunged into the bewildering world of Indian politics.

Part One
Autumn

One

I was stiff and my limbs ached. I had been sitting cross-legged since dawn, working my way through a tray of apricot stones, sorting the kernels from the cracked shells. In the courtyard around me four or five nuns were busy, some raking out barley grain to dry in the sun, others crushing and kneading the kernels of the apricot stones to extract their oil. I seemed to have slipped easily into the rhythm of life at Julichang. The days followed a similar pattern and were filled with work.

It was now October and the chill of the morning air warned us that the short summer was almost over. Winter approached. From my arrival, almost a month earlier, I had sensed the nuns' anxiety as they hastened to complete all their outdoor tasks in advance of the severe frosts. Cultivation was difficult and it had to be tightly squeezed into the months between May and September. In addition to sorting the piles of apricot stones, the nuns planned to clear the vegetable plots and to prepare as much grain as possible, washing, drying, roasting and, finally, grinding it into flour, before the river became covered with ice.

Ladakh, lying high on the Central Asian plateau, is inhospitable in its climate and terrain. Temperatures are extreme and the atmosphere is dry. Travelling by bus across the country to Julichang, I had looked out over an expanse of rocky, desert landscape which was barely broken, except here and there as clusters of vegetation indicated human settlement. The local people only knew two seasons, summer and winter, and the sharp division between them was mirrored in the contrast between outdoor and indoor work. But the short periods of transition were times of great activity and the nuns at Julichang, pressed and harried, were glad to use an extra pair of hands, delegating to me plenty of the tedious, unskilled jobs.

We began our tasks at first light. The cook, Sonam, rose early and went down to the river to draw water for the day's cooking; then, one by one, the other nuns emerged. From my sleeping place on the roof of the nunnery, I heard the quiet recitation of prayers as the women moved about outside, sweeping the courtyard and stoking the small fire which kept a pot of tea warm throughout the day.

Usually I hurried into the kitchen. It was strategically placed, situated at the top of the nunnery above the courtyard, and its windows looked out on to the footpath which linked the monastery and village with the Leh road. The ferocious barking of the dog tethered below, at the entrance to Julichang, always alerted us to visitors; and, by peeping through the wooden shutters, we were able to catch a first glimpse of those approaching.

In the early morning, however, the shutters were tightly closed against the cold air and the kitchen was dark and smoky. A wood stove stood in the centre of the floor, dominating the interior. It was moulded from a particular kind of river-bed clay, but, black and highly polished, it appeared at first sight to have been made from cast iron. It did not have a chimney and the smoke from the fire was drawn out, somewhat erratically, through a small hole in the roof.

Before setting off for the river, Sonam used her goat-skin bellows to ignite the embers which lay in the bottom of the stove; but often, when unattended, the fire smouldered and I entered a kitchen filled with acrid wood smoke. I crouched close to the stove, sometimes blowing on the twigs in a vain effort to get it going, and listened for the sound of Sonam's slow, heavy footsteps. Eventually she appeared, almost bent double beneath the weight of the jerry can, and we struggled to unload it from her back, decanting most of the water into large iron buckets. Carrying water up from the river was one task I simply wasn't strong enough to undertake; but Sonam barely paused for breath on her return, turning her attention immediately to the fire which she built up beneath the pot of soup cooking for our breakfast.

During the summer and early autumn the thin, barley flour soup was fortified with turnips or swedes from Julichang's garden and these vegetables were particularly savoured because they were available for only a few months of the year.

The women did not sit down together as a community for breakfast; rather, Sonam carried small pots filled with broth into the courtyard where most of the nuns were already at work. Sonam and I ate our soup in the kitchen and she busied herself with the food preparations for the day. She began with milking.

The herd of cattle and the few goats kept at Julichang supplied milk for both monastery and nunnery, but much of it was churned into butter. Butter was consumed in considerable amounts in tea and it also had important religious uses. The elaborate altars in the temples and monastic cells at Rizong were constructed from different offerings; prominent among them were butter lamps and dough effigies decorated with shapes moulded out of butter. Once Sonam had finished milking she herded the animals into the woods where they foraged in the dry undergrowth for clumps of sparse vegetation and she returned, with heavy pails, to the kitchen.

While Sonam was absent, I remained indoors tending the fire and reading religious texts which neither she nor the other nuns had time to do. The women were surprised and delighted when they discovered that I could read Tibetan. It became my responsibility in the community to begin the day in this way. Every morning I unwrapped the layers of coarse cloth, blackened through exposure to smoke from the wood stove, to reveal beneath further layers of delicate silk brocade which covered a set of fragile hand-printed scripts. Aside from her robes, rosary beads and wooden bowl, these papers were the cook's only possessions and she entrusted them to me.

From my place at the fireside, the texts carefully balanced across my knees, I looked up every now and then as Sonam drew my attention to different stages in the process of making tea. Already her cheeks were streaked with soot and her brow furrowed with concentration as she measured out the correct quantities of butter, salt, and tea. With short, grunting sounds she set to work, vigorously blending the ingredients in a long wooden churn before pouring the frothing liquid into the heavy iron pot which she heated on the stove. Beckoning me to the fireside, Sonam invited me to sample the tea; but I knew immediately from her open, expressive face whether she was satisfied or not and before I could offer my cautious opinion she had usually adjusted its taste with a pinch more salt or a

ladle of water. Sometimes the tea tasted rancid and bitter; at
other times it was rich and smooth and I quickly learned that
it was the quality of the butter which was critical in determin-
ing the flavour of the tea. With Sonam's expert guidance,
though, I soon felt confident in my judgment of different kinds
of tea and I often amused people by offering my comments on
the quality of a particular pot. I had been warned in advance
about Ladakhi butter tea, but luckily from the beginning I had
liked it. I was fortunate, since hospitality in Ladakh always
involved the serving of tea and I found myself having to drink
great quantities of it. At frequent intervals throughout the day
the nuns would break the monotony of their work by serving
tea; and they always kept a pot warming on the hearth in case
of visitors.

Sonam and I found it easy to work together in the kitchen.
She seemed to enjoy showing me how to do some of the sim-
pler tasks and I learned fast, benefiting from her close supervision and careful instructions which she would keep on
repeating until she was sure that I had understood her. Usually
she dispatched me with the first pot of tea. Somewhat reluctantly I left the warmth of the kitchen, carrying it to the
women outside in the courtyard; and then I went back to my
job of sorting the apricot stones. By now it was mid-morning,
but the sun's rays had not yet penetrated the deep narrow
valley which housed Julichang; until midday they rarely
reached the compound where we worked. I sat close to Urgen,
working between him and Chuski. Urgen cracked the stones
open and heaped them into small piles around him. I collected
up handfuls and, spreading them out across a smooth wooden
tray, I began to separate the shells from the kernels. The
broken shells were sharp and very soon the tips of my fingers
felt tender and sore. For this task I wore gloves with half-fin-
gers which enabled me to work quickly despite the chill of the
morning air. The nuns had never seen such gloves before and
they admired them as being perfectly suited to my task.

At first I was surprised to find a man living at the nunnery.
Urgen sat day after day in a corner of the courtyard, cracking
stones and chuckling at his own jokes which he told to the
nuns working nearby. I could never understand them; but I
liked the sound of the lively banter he provoked. Urgen was
crippled. His legs were useless and bound up beneath him, his

grey coat was stained with beer and its hem badly frayed because of the way he dragged himself along the ground on a pair of makeshift wooden crutches. Urgen worked with the nuns during the summer; in the winter months he became a tailor for the monastery. As the days grew cooler and the sun took longer to fill the courtyard, Urgen began to look forward to leaving for Rizong. One day several of the young monks came to Julichang and hoisted him on to the back of a donkey which carried him up the steep mountain path. I found his departure left the nunnery a quiet, subdued place, and although I encountered his sharp wit again on the occasions we worked together at Rizong, he never seemed quite the same bold, jocular figure as when he was in the company of the nuns.

It was difficult to glean any personal details about Urgen; he was reluctant to talk about his past and the nuns themselves were vague about his origins and about how he had come to live in the valley. I came across others who, for one reason or another, had taken refuge at Julichang and whose readiness to shoulder some of the burden of work guaranteed their integration into the community. Gradually I realized that this was the key to my own acceptance by the nuns.

After sifting through my tray, I passed the apricot kernels to Chuski, the nun responsible for extracting their oil. She crouched low on the ground, kneading and pressing the kernels against a long, sloping stone which was scooped out at the bottom. I watched the oil as it dribbled down and collected in the cup. It was slow, strenuous work, but there was skill and gracefulness in Chuski's movements. Frequently, she paused to rest and, pushing back her hat which slipped forward over her brow, she smiled shyly at me. Her face softened and its puckered lines disappeared to reveal a different woman from the one I had seen a moment ago. At first glance Chuski looked like most of the other women at Julichang. She wore a thick woollen skirt sewn from strips of cloth and a long shawl, which she carefully arranged over her shoulders to cover the sleeveless bodice beneath. These red robes and her shaven head were symbols of admission to the monastic life, and they marked Chuski's renunciation of worldly possessions and her observation of a vow of celibacy. The many layers of heavy clothes which the nuns wore emphasized their solid, rugged physiques and, although I followed their example in adapting my own dress to the harsh conditions, I could not disguise the feebleness of my limbs. Chuski's body was strong and sturdy and appeared to have been built to withstand the constant demands of manual labour; but, the strain of working in the difficult Himalayan conditions marked everyone, and it showed in her haggard, drawn face. When Chuski rested, though, her appearance could change. Her features were less sharply defined and her skin seemed to soften over fuller, rounder cheeks, crinkling in delicate folds around her eyes. Sometimes she looked girlish, her face open and smiling; at other times Chuski retreated behind a gentle, rather dreamy expression which I could not penetrate.

At the end of the day I helped Chuski gather up the dross remaining after the oil had been extracted. It was used as cattle fodder during the winter months and we added the day's left overs to those which already filled several old metal cans. We also swept up the empty shells of the apricot stones, since these too were kept for the winter when they were burned as fuel. I was fascinated by the intricacy of the work methods and the inventiveness of the women. Although I was keen to share the burden of chores, I knew the limitations of my own abilities and I was quick to join in the laughter which my clumsiness provoked among the nuns. Cracking apricot stones looked easy enough; but when I tried, I invariably shattered the kernel inside and then I would have to get on my hands and knees to search the dusty floor in order to retrieve the fragments. On other occasions I entertained everyone in the courtyard when I tried my hand at churning tea or making dough and would find, in no time at all, that I had splattered my face and hair with butter or flour.

Sonam spent the morning alone in the kitchen where she prepared the main meal of the day. The food was always the same – a heavy, dark porridge (which I detested) and shredded radish. It was the only time when we all sat down together; and it marked the beginning of the fast, observed by most of the nuns until the following morning. I noticed that the women ate almost continuously until then – scraps of bread, cold porridge, walnuts, dried apricots, all of which they kept wrapped in cloth in the front pouch of their robes. The food looked very unappetizing when they pulled it out, hard and stale; but, before long, I found myself doing the same, storing scraps and relishing, weeks later, each piece down to the last crumb.

Often our lunch in the courtyard was interrupted by the arrival of monks from Rizong. Usually it was the bursar with some of the young boys, novices, on whom he depended to carry supplies of milk and butter back up the mountainside. At other times he was accompanied by two or three senior monks. Hurrying to make space for their visitors beside the tiny hearth, the nuns cut short their rest from work and returned to their tasks. While we toiled, the monks sat around the fire, reading religious texts and planning what chores were to be undertaken at the nunnery in the future. I soon learned that everything we did at Julichang was under the supervision and control of the monastery. We were only one part of Rizong's empire which drew the nunnery, and several villages and far-flung monastic communities into a complex system of production and exchange. Rizong's economic affairs were managed by a council of senior monks headed by the bursar. The post of bursar conferred immense power on the holder, but the responsibilities were heavy. It was a position not eagerly sought by the monks since it required a mastery of all the intricacies of the monastic economy and it involved constant travelling on foot and horseback between the different settlements which supplied goods and labour to Rizong. The post circulated among the monks and, after some years service, the incumbent expected to be relieved of his duties and permitted to return to religious devotion. Smiling broadly, the bursar liked to stand over me as I sorted stones in the courtyard. He obviously took delight in the ease with which I had adapted to the work pattern of the nunnery and he was quick to include me in his future plans.

On most days I worked outdoors until the late afternoon. By then the sun had disappeared behind the steep valley wall and the nunnery was left once more in shadow. Blowing gently, a light breeze began to whip up the dust around the courtyard and it warned us that dusk was closing in. For me, it signalled that it was time to climb the path to Rizong and bring down the cattle for evening milking.

This had been the responsibility of Dondrup. She was a curious woman, rather like Urgen, who had lived at the nunnery for many years, but no one seemed to know where she had come from or what circumstances had caused her to make Julichang her home. I was told that she was a *chomo*. This meant she had not taken formal monastic vows, but she lived a celibate life, shaved her head and wore red clothes (but not robes). Although I knew of the ambivalence which surrounded the status of nuns within Buddhism, I hadn't realized how rare ordained nuns actually were until I visited Ladakh. *Chomo* were a striking expression of the historical marginality of women within monastic Buddhism. They were a common sight in the Himalayas and the majority lived in the household of their parents or brothers where they were treated more or less as domestic servants. Occasionally these women were attached to monasteries. They cooked for the monks and took responsibility for the cleaning and upkeep of the temples. I heard many jokes about *chomo*, women thought to be unmarriageable or "old maids", and, at first, I was amused to discover that I was considered to be one in this context. But, from the beginning, it was a role which I felt comfortable with. I readily adapted myself to the expectations associated with such a position and gradually the sense of my having any special status which might distinguish me from the other women at Julichang diminished.

I found it very difficult to guess Dondrup's age. Her face was weathered and deeply lined, the dehydrated skin drooped in folds around a sunken mouth and her expression was habitually dour. She shuffled along, muttering to herself, always grumbling; but, sometimes, when she was teased, her face could break into a wide and impish, toothless grin. Dondrup was now slow and tired and she was grateful when I offered to take over the daily chore of climbing the mountainside to retrieve the cattle.

Setting out along the footpath to the monastery, I followed, at first, the course of the river and cut through the dense woodland which stretched down to the water. Here among the trees I usually came across Sonam, scouring the ground for dried dung and twigs which she could burn in the kitchen stove. She tossed them into the conical basket strapped to her back, and would return to Julichang only when it was piled high with fuel. If I expected to bring back supplies from Rizong I carried a similar basket; but, fortunately, it was empty and light on my ascent. The first part of the path was gently sloping but once I reached a fork in the path marked by a small shrine and prayer stones, I took a sharp left turn and began the steep climb to the monastery; to continue along the river would lead me to Lababs, a small settlement of *chomo* and eventually to the village of Yangthang beyond.

I began to leave the woods behind, making my way slowly through the dry valley. No matter how carefully I conserved my energy, the altitude never failed to exhaust me and I was forced to rest partway up the mountainside. The path was steep and winding and enclosed by high walls. It was impossible to see the monastery until the last moment.

Suddenly the narrow valley opened out and ahead lay Rizong. The first glimpse returned me to the picture I had carried in my mind for many months before I arrived in Ladakh. It had been formed by my reading an account, given by a European traveller, of his journey through the Himalayas in the 1930s. He wrote:

A few more turns – the Yellow Lama still pranced along in front of us, now appearing, now disappearing in the windings of the narrow gorge – and then, suddenly Rizong, amazing, theatrical . . . when the door of the largest temple was opened for us and when we went into a place frescoed with paintings and adorned with *tanca* [silk wall-hangings depicting deities of the Tibetan pantheon], in which the long rows of little lamps lighted in honour of the divinities did not break a twilight full of mystery and meditation, when we saw the lamas inside, in two long rows on the ground, repeating their eternal prayer, intoning it on one note, accompanied by the muffled beat of a drum . . . certainly at that moment, one could not be unconscious of the deep feeling of mysticism which seemed to emanate from the walls, from the light, from the very air perfumed with benzoin and from those calm, indifferent, inspired, ascetic men.

For a long time I had looked for descriptions of Rizong monastery. The year before, while living in another part of the Himalayas, I had been told that a community of nuns was attached to the foundation; but it seemed impossible to acquire any accurate information. People told me that they had heard others talk of nuns at Rizong, though no one seemed sure that a nunnery existed; so when, at last, I happened upon this description of Rizong, I found myself easily drawn into the writer's sense of adventure and discovery. I was encouraged to seek out more details concerning the monastery's foundation a century earlier and, although the accounts I located mixed history with myth and legend, I absorbed them eagerly and stored them in my memory.

I learned that Tsultim Nyima, a wealthy merchant from Saspol, a small settlement on the banks of the Indus river, was crossing the mountains on horseback with goods from Tibet. Tired and thirsty, he took shelter in a deep, dry valley which had a sheer wall of rock rising to the north. At the base of the gorge, stretching away to the south, he dug a hole so that water would collect and enable his horses to drink.

On the return journey, the merchant noticed that water had sprung in the hole even though he knew there had been no rain. Interpreting this as an auspicious sign he performed a small Buddhist ceremony on the spot and vowed to found a monastery there. At the time, the remote rocky valley was uninhabited and the merchant was able to claim great areas of land for the monastery. He recruited labour for the construction of the buildings and settled villagers in the adjacent valley. Their descendants, the inhabitants of Yangthang, continued to provide labour, services, and material support to Rizong.

Tsultim Nyima, being childless, consulted a senior lama in an effort to be blessed with offspring. He was told that the lama foresaw his own approaching death and that he would be reborn as the merchant's son. In due course a son was born, named Shas, and later he became one of the two abbots of Rizong. With the completion of the building, Tsultim Nyima was ordained as the first novice and over seventy monks joined the community. The line of the merchant continued through named incarnations, regularly occupying the position of second abbot of the monastery. Until 1959 and the flight of the Dalai Lama into exile, Rizong maintained close ties with major monasteries in Tibet, its monks and abbots frequently journeying there, across the mountains to receive instruction and training in matters of Buddhist doctrine. As a community, it enjoyed a reputation for scholarship, discipline and spiritual integrity.

Rizong now stood before me. It was built into a sheer rock-face; its whitewashed buildings were constructed in a step-like formation, with the temples and suites of the two head lamas situated in the upper levels. Below were the kitchen and store-rooms of the bursar and a maze of small cells occupied by individual monks.

The monastery was virtually deserted at this time of year. Its abbots had long since abandoned Rizong; they lived in one of the Tibetan refugee settlements in southern India and only occasionally made summer visits to Ladakh. In the autumn many of the other monks were away, trading in distant places or supervising work in the different villages. They did not return until the festival of Namgyal Stonchok which marked the onset of winter and the beginning of an important religious season.

If the bursar or the boys saw me approaching, they waved from one of the balconies and watched me as I struggled to climb up the last and steepest half-mile. Again I was forced to rest, before threading my way along the narrow passages to the bursar's quarters. I was conscious of the low murmuring of prayers and, although the sounds barely broke the silence, their strange, haunting tone reminded me that I was outside the monastery's world of mystery and meditation.

Usually, the bursar invited me to take tea with him on the verandah outside his storerooms. He hurried out from his rooms, carrying a low wooden table and a faded Tibetan rug for me to sit on, and he shouted to one of the young monks in the kitchen below to bring a pot of freshly made tea. The view from his balcony was magnificent. I never tired of looking across the wide valley and over the dry, brown-grey landscape to the rows of dark mountains in the far distance. The changing light in the late afternoon cast eerie shadows over the rough terrain. Many times I watched the movement of heavy snow-clouds as they floated and swirled, before descending and obscuring the sharp line of peaks against the sky. I began to sense the ferocity of a Himalayan winter.

Resting in the cool afternoon air, I had a chance to catch my breath before climbing the higher slopes where the cattle grazed. It was also a good opportunity to ask the bursar about his work, for I was very curious to discover more about the scale and complexity of Rizong's operations. I knew he occupied a difficult position. He was regarded with ambivalence by both the nuns and villagers, because he was the personification of the heavy demands made upon their time and other scarce resources by the monastery. But I had noticed too, that the bursar's reputation for meanness was not wholly undeserved. From my own experience, I knew how he always begrudged parting with any of the items the nuns asked me to bring back to Julichang.

I never forgot the first glimpse I had of his storerooms. They were filled with goods, to the point of overflowing. Standing in the doorway of the main room I looked over a floor covered with mounds of butter and cheese, sacks of tea, rice and white sugar, dried apricots, and walnuts. Fleeces hung from the ceiling and goat skins from the walls. Many of these were luxury items, scarce in Ladakh and almost never seen in the villages or at the nunnery, because they could be acquired only by cash purchase or through long-distance trade. So full was this room that everything seemed to be heaped together in a jumbled mass; but I had no doubt that the bursar, in his meticulous and miserly way, would know to the last item where everything was and how much was stored.

Sometimes, though, if he was feeling particularly generous, the bursar filled my hands with apricots, sweet kernels, or walnuts and I hurriedly stuffed them into the pouch of my coat before he could change his mind. Later I shared them out among the nuns and Dondrup. The women were amused by my ability to charm such delicacies out of a reluctant bursar and soon they relied on me to make requests on their behalf for supplies from the monastery.

By dusk the cattle were high above Rizong in search of isolated scraps of vegetation. I scrambled up the steep slopes of loose rock to reach them, keeping my eye fixed firmly on where they were and not daring to look behind at the sheer mountainside falling away below me. As I drew near, the cows began to descend, slithering and skidding almost vertically down the scree. My descent was much more cautious and I zigzagged slowly, afraid of losing my footing and tumbling helplessly all the way back to the monastery. Relieved, I returned to the safety of the path. Already the cattle were ahead of me, pushing, jostling and trotting as they followed the familiar route to Julichang. When we emerged from the dry valley, I often found Dondrup waiting beside the shrine to ensure that the herd did not scatter at the fork in the track and disappear into the woodland.

It was almost dark and I returned to Julichang as the tasks in the courtyard were being completed for the day. There was just enough light, however, for the nuns to be able to read from their scriptures. This short period of time, squeezed tightly between dusk and night, was the only opportunity the women had for religious practice. After darkness fell, the nuns could continue to read with the aid of a dim, oil lamp; but this was rare. Kerosene was scarce and had to be requested from the bursar. I always found it a strange interlude as I watched the fading profiles of the women, their tired, grimy faces blurring in the thick grey dusk, while their voices seemed to become stronger and more distinctive, the sound of their prayers ringing through the night air.

Sonam could not join us in the courtyard; she was still hard at work, milking the cattle and goats. Later we heard her calling from the kitchen. Wearily, Dondrup stirred and shuffled across the dark courtyard to fasten the animals in the shed for the night. I followed, making my way to the kitchen where I spent the evening with Sonam.

Every other night we made butter. Milk was not so plentiful as in the summer, when butter was often churned twice a day, but the monastery still needed its regular quota. For this purpose the bursar gave Sonam a supply of candles to be used in the kitchen after dark. Butter was made using a handcut wooden whisk, secured to a post in the middle of the kitchen. The whisk, kept upright in the barrel of milk and yoghurt, had a length of rope wound around its stem. By pulling first with the left hand, next with the right, the milk was slowly churned. The cook and I took turns sitting in front of the barrel, pulling the heavy whisk one way and then the other. We counted and agreed to change over after fifty pulls. Before long we knew exactly how many rotations were required before the milk turned, and this was the way I learned to count in Ladakhi. Finally, there was a rush to add boiling water at just the right moment, to solidify the curds. The freshly made butter was covered and left to stand overnight.

It was several hours work, but Sonam, who often did not observe the daily fast, prepared a meal which we ate when we had finished churning. She enjoyed being the nunnery's cook and she wanted me to try all the different dishes of Ladakh. Despite her very limited range of ingredients – vegetables, spices, barley flour, and occasionally rice – she never failed to produce anything less than an excellent cuisine. Her great achievement as a cook derived largely from the many ways she devised to disguise barley flour. Some evenings she rolled long, thin strips of dough which resembled pasta; at other times, she moulded it into different shapes and served them in a highly spiced sauce. My favourite was a dish of vegetables, mainly swedes, which contained dough pieces, each one carefully modelled by Sonam to resemble the shape of donkeys' ears.

From my first days at Julichang I found Sonam to be a loyal friend. I was at ease in her company and she was kind and protective to me as I struggled to become familiar with the language and with the daily routine of the nuns. I had liked her immediately; her direct manner, reflected in her alert, handsome face which broke so easily into a smile, her animated way of speaking – but, above all, I liked her irrepressible curiosity. In the evenings, squatting around the kitchen fire, we went over the day's events and Sonam told me who the visitors were, where they came from, what they were doing. She was very familiar with affairs in the village and at the monastery, since the nunnery was an important staging-post for travellers and the kitchen a focal point for the exchange of news and gossip. Sonam's skills and temperament qualified her perfectly for this role. She was seemingly tireless, and I often marvelled at the speed with which she moved between the different tasks filling her day and evening; and yet despite the endless round of work, she still found reserves of good humour and hospitality with which to welcome visitors to the nunnery. She rested only rarely; and then I would see her crouching on her haunches at the fireside as she snatched a few mouthfuls of tea or soup.

At night Sonam pulled a few coarse rugs over herself and curled up beside the kitchen stove. I would stumble into the darkness outside and climb the wooden ladder which led up on to the nunnery roof where I slept.

Two

To the nuns I was a curiosity, but I did not feel an outsider. I began to find a place and a role in this remote Buddhist nunnery. Until that moment I had always been sceptical of people who claimed to have been truly at home in another culture; but here, for the first time, I experienced an ease, a sense of belonging which led me to believe that I could become part of the community of religious women.

Sometimes I cast my mind back over the previous year when I had set out from Cambridge, as an anthropologist, my head filled with history and abstract notions of Buddhism culled from books. My interest in the philosophy and practice of Tibetan Buddhism was recent and rather academic. It seemed to have grown in a vague way from my desire to escape the confines of intellectual life and yet, as I soon found out, I remained trapped within them, preparing to study the meaning of scriptural knowledge in another society. Perhaps I could trace deeper roots in my personal history, returning to one of my earliest memories of childhood, that of running my hands over the smooth, polished surface of the wooden Burmese Buddha with broken fingers, which stood by the door of the museum near my home. If there was an anchor in my past, that familiar meditative pose of the Buddha lodged in my memory as an image of the contemplative life; and it was reinforced, initially, by everything I learned. But the experience of living at Julichang turned upside down my bookish notions of spirituality.

I had begun by studying various historical accounts of Buddhism and I was drawn to the simple, yet profound, truths which lay at its core. I read that Gautama, the Buddha, was born during the fifth century BC in Kapilavastu, a town lying on the border between India and Nepal. His early life was sheltered and he grew up shielded from the world by the wealth and status of his family. Later he married and his wife bore him a son. One day, driving beyond the walls of his palace, Gautama was deeply affected by the sight, first, of an old man; then, of a sick man; and, finally, of a corpse being carried to the cremation ground. He reflected on the aversion he felt:

But is this right? I also am subject to decay, and am not free from the power of old age, sickness and death. Is it right that I should feel horror, repulsion, and disgust when I see another in such a plight? And when I reflected thus, all the joy of life, which there is in life, died within me.

Gautama saw, too, an ascetic holy man and he resolved to follow his example, by renouncing the world and embarking on a search for immortality.

At the age of twenty-nine, Gautama left his family and household life to become a wandering mendicant. For six years he contemplated the problems of existence, seeking to attain wisdom through forest dwelling, yogic practice, meditation, fasting, and other extreme forms of asceticism. Physical mortification, however, did not bring about the knowledge and insight he sought, and, to the disappointment of his companions, Gautama abandoned the severe austerities he had practised. He made his way to the Deer Park at Sarnath, near Benares and, after bathing and taking nourishment, he sat alone beneath the *bodhi* tree.

Here he meditated, passing through different stages of concentration, purifying his mind. He contemplated his former lives, the death and rebirth of beings, and the nature of desire and suffering. During the course of a night Gautama penetrated the truth and was thereby set free from the fetters of mortal existence. He became Buddha, the Enlightened One.

For some weeks the Buddha continued to meditate, before expounding the Dharma or Doctrine to the handful of mendicants who had sought spiritual insight with him. These teachings began with the Buddha's enunciation of the Middle Way: the Noble Eightfold Path to salvation (right views, right intention, right speech, right action, right livelihood, right effort, right mindfulness, right concentration) which avoided both extremes of self-indulgence and self-denial. The Four Noble Truths followed: all existence is suffering (*samsara*, the endless cycle of rebirth in which the form of suffering is dependent on past actions, positive or negative karma); the origin of suffering (attachment, craving, ignorance); the cessation of suffering (salvation, release from *samsara*, nirvana); the way to the cessation of suffering (the Noble Eightfold Path). The Buddha also taught his disciples the Doctrine of no-self, that there is no soul, no permanent, stable, enduring ego or "I", but merely a fluctuating, transitory group of five elements (form, feeling, perception, volition, and consciousness). It is when the individual is freed from attachment and ignorance, impelling these different elements to be reborn, that he achieves emancipation and enlightenment. For the next forty-five years the Buddha travelled extensively. He gave teachings and he founded a community of monks.

From the beginning, though, I faced a contradiction in my reading of these historical accounts. The place of women seemed ambiguous. I remembered the conversation between Gautama, the Buddha, and Ananda, one of his disciples. When Ananda first asked, "How are we monks to behave when we see women?" Gautama replied, "Don't see them."

"But if we should see them, what are we to do?"

"Don't speak to them."

"What if they speak to us, what then?"

"Let your thoughts be fixed in deep meditation."

But I also knew that women were prominent among the early, lay disciples of the Buddha. I read that they attended his public teachings and, in wishing to devote themselves fully to the spiritual life, they had sought admission to the religious order. At first their request was refused. It was said that in the fifth year of the Buddha's teaching, his aunt Mahapajapati and five hundred women, their heads shaven, dressed in yellow robes, requested permission to leave household life and to go forth to become nuns. Again their request was turned down. Three times, deputations of women approached the Buddha and each time their petition for admission was rejected. Eventually, after the intervention of Ananda, the Buddha reluctantly agreed to open the order to women on the condition that Mahapajapati and her companions agreed to be bound by the Eight Chief Rules, devised specifically for women. These rules constituted their initiation and placed the women in a subordinate position within the community.

Just as with men, the monastic order in ancient Buddhism was open to all women. It was celibacy after admission, not virginity, which was required of entrants. Widows, wives and even prostitutes could seek entry. Neither dowry nor wealth was required of prospective novices. It was difficult, however, for women to use the order as an escape or refuge from particular domestic problems, since they had to have the approval of their father or husband and the two-year novicehood tested their dedication. On the other hand, parents could not easily relieve themselves of daughters who had mental or physical blemishes. A series of questions was drawn up in the admission procedure to preserve the integrity of the order.

The lives of the early Buddhist nuns resembled those of the monks. They rose before dawn to meditate. A period was set aside in the morning for the alms round, when they passed through the streets accepting food placed in their begging bowls by householders seeking to earn merit. The single meal of the day was taken at noon. Thereafter the women were engaged in meditation, study and teachings. For most of the year, the nuns travelled, following the Buddha, attending sermons, observing the rain retreat and other days set aside in each month for confession.

In their spiritual endeavours, the female devotees were dependent on monks for ceremonial leadership; and, in their organization, they lacked final authority over their affairs. Discipline was tight and over five hundred restrictions and regulations bound their lives.

My reading carried me far and wide, through the labyrinth of Buddhism's long and complex history into strange, remote places where the faith merged with existing beliefs and practices to create exotic local forms. I was attracted, like many other people, to the colourful Tibetan tradition with its crowded pantheon of gods and demons; its striking iconography and temple ritual; its scholars, hermits, and magicians. Moreover, femininity was a prominent feature of this world, since at the core of the philosophy and practice of Tibetan Buddhism lay the union of male and female principles, wisdom and compassion. Tibet became the symbol of an integrated spiritual experience, and the penetration of the wild, inaccessible Himalayan terrain was the beginning of my journey into its mystical heartland.

Before arriving at Julichang I had spent some months in Dharmsala, a small hill-station in the Himalayas where the Tibetan spiritual leader, the Dalai Lama, lived in exile. Here I started to study the language and religion; but, from the beginning, it was the ambiguity associated with the place of women within Buddhism which fuelled my interest. I sought to uncover the meaning of the religious life for women, but the more I delved the harder it seemed to grasp. First of all, nuns themselves were nowhere to be seen. They were as invisible and as elusive as they had become in the historical records and accounts of Buddhism I studied. Whenever I raised my interest in the lives of Buddhist nuns I was laughed at. I didn't seem to realize that they had no status at all. No one took them seriously. I was frequently told that nuns "played" at being religious devotees, but in reality they were frustrated, gossiping women. It soon became clear to me that they were mocked by all sections of society.

Eventually I located a small group of nuns in Dharmsala and, from a place at the back of the temple, I witnessed the cycle of Buddhist ceremonies, the succession of religious observances which made up each day, each month, each year. I felt the power and intensity of each ritual occasion; I marvelled at the intricacy of the practices and the exotic sights and sounds of the temple; but, at the end of every ceremony, the women were still the same – unaffected, distant, ordinary. I blamed my own insensitivity, my linguistic incompetence, my failure to understand the texts. I spent almost a year with these women; I observed and gathered facts; but I remained an outsider looking on.

I wasn't going to be so easily deterred and I decided to try again. My interest had been caught by Ladakh, a remote Buddhist kingdom lying to the north of Dharmsala. In former times, it had been the market place for Central Asia, and goods carried along the ancient silk and spice routes found their way into the streets of its capital, Leh. It was along these trade routes, too, that Mahayana Buddhism had been carried into Ladakh during the early centuries of the Christian era.

The definitive form of Buddhism, however, emerged much later, largely as a consequence of the political strife in neighbouring Tibet. During the ninth-century reign of the Tibetan king, Glangdarma, the religion was suppressed and many influential scholars took refuge in Ladakh, establishing monastic orders there. Although the later history of Buddhism in Tibet was characterized by a proliferation of different schools, each vying with one another for religious and temporal supremacy, a measure of internal stability followed the reforms of Tsongkhapa. This great Tibetan scholar founded the Yellow Hat school in the fourteenth century. It quickly became the dominant school, achieving its final consolidation of power with the establishment of the office of the Dalai Lama. Several monasteries subsequently founded in Ladakh adhered to the reformed, or Yellow Hat, sect. Their monks maintained close links with teachers and scholars in Lhasa, the spiritual capital of the region. Following the Chinese invasion of Tibet in 1959, Ladakh found itself once more assuming the guardianship of the Buddhist faith in the Himalayas.

During my stay in Dharmsala, I occasionally saw Ladakhi monks in the market square. They were distinctive in their dress and speech; and their appearance invariably provoked comment or laughter from Tibetans who considered them coarse and uncivilized. Despite warnings about the harshness of Ladakh's climate and terrain and the uncertainty as to whether I would be allowed to visit the area, since much of the country was closed for reasons of security, I decided to try and find the nunnery I had heard about. It was thought to be situated beneath Rizong, lying in a dark, narrow gorge and renowned for a magnificent summer crop of apricots which gave the nunnery its name, Julichang. To my good fortune, one of the nuns from Dharmsala was planning to travel to Leh and she offered to accompany me to Julichang.

As we set out, the exhilaration of adventure returned. By now I had more or less abandoned any pretension to being an anthropologist. From the beginning it was a role I had never really identified with; it seemed an anachronism, too closely associated for comfort with a colonial past and with the dubious adventures of intrepid male explorers. Although as a student I had read a great deal of anthropological literature, I wasn't so sure what was involved in "being an anthropologist", since anthropologists took great care to mask or remove their presence from the accounts they wrote about human society. Indeed it was nearly impossible to find anyone in Cambridge who was willing to talk about their own experience of fieldwork. It was regarded as an initiation process, the details of which were kept secret; and I found that almost everyone who underwent this rite of passage was prepared to collude in maintaining an atmosphere of mystery. I suppose it enhanced their sense of achievement or covered up a lingering sense of personal inadequacy.

The only thing I knew with any confidence was the importance of notebooks. Anthropologists talked a good deal about their field notes and readily recounted various nightmares in which these books were nearly lost or destroyed. Packing a set in my rucksack, I tried hard to imagine what it would feel like to fill up the pages; but it was not long after I arrived in the Himalayas, facing long, empty days, that I realized what a refuge the collection of facts could become. Eventually, I stopped trying to amass endless details of ceremonial ritual: perhaps I suspected that it was leading me in the wrong direction. Even so, when I left Dharmsala and gave away all my unused notebooks, I did it with a sense of professional failure. In retrospect, however, it was an important first step as I struggled to discard the intellectual trappings which prevented me from seeing much of what was around me. In shrugging off the limitations of that role, I found myself entering another world, one which I could never have imagined.

Three

During my first weeks at Julichang I often found it difficult to follow the unfamiliar Ladakhi dialect spoken by the nuns. I withdrew from the conversations around me in the courtyard and became absorbed in watching the women carrying out their tasks. I tried to form some impression of their different characters, noting distinctive facial expressions and body movements and storing in my memory the individual sounds of the nuns' voices. The pictures which crystallized in my mind were originally inseparable from the routines of work that shaped our lives, for this was how I came to know the women.

I watched Tsultim, hurrying between the courtyard, the woods and the nunnery storerooms. She was in charge of the preparation and storage of grain. This absorbed a great deal of her energy in the short weeks of autumn because barley flour, the staple of our diet, had to be stockpiled for the long winter months. She depended on us to help her. We readily put aside our own work to spend time washing the grain, or turning it as it dried in the sun, or sweeping it into piles for roasting and grinding; but we hurried because already sacks of grain were beginning to arrive at the nunnery from other settlements attached to Rizong.

Every year a group of representatives from these villages held a meeting with the bursar and negotiated what amount of newly harvested grain they would pay to the monastery as rent. Most of it was collected from the outlying villages and was brought to Julichang by pairs of men who came from nearby Yangthang. Each journey took two days. In order to make an early start for Saspol or Hemis Shugba, the men left their households in the late afternoon and spent the first evening at the nunnery. At daybreak they set out with four or five cattle across the mountains and after the long trek they rested overnight in the village, returning to Julichang at dusk the following day. Their arrival was always signalled by a loud commotion outside the nunnery. Barking angrily, the dog alerted us to the approach of the party; then we heard the men, shouting above the noise, as they tried to steer the heavily laden animals through the entrance to the nunnery. Quickly we abandoned our tasks in the courtyard. I followed the nuns outside and we helped to stack the bags of grain in the storerooms ready for washing the next morning.

The Yangthang villagers were paying labour tribute, owed to the monastery. They took turns to undertake the journeys and when they stayed overnight at the nunnery, Sonam cooked a meal for them and we sat together in the kitchen, talking late into the evening. I came to know a number of them well. They gossiped about village affairs and Sonam always pressed them to tell her what they had heard in the other settlements. There was usually news to relay about marriages being arranged, about illness and death; sometimes there was the anticipation of the arrival of a Buddhist scholar to a nearby monastery or discussion of the whereabouts of particular monks. When I became more familiar with the dialect I was able to join in the conversation; but more often I listened as the older men grumbled about the bursar and complained about the burden of work demanded by the monastery. It was difficult for them to fulfil these religious obligations at a time when they were under considerable pressure in the village to finish work before the onset of winter.

The land in Yangthang on which they raised crops and kept cattle belonged to Rizong. In return the villagers paid rent to the monastery. It consisted of labour service, and a quantity of goods they produced from the fields. The villagers were caught in a complex web of religious and economic obligations, and these ties with Rizong were cemented by the tradition of offering a number of young village boys to the monastery for religious instruction.

I knew that the men who were transporting grain resented being away from Yangthang at one of the busiest times of the year. Winter was now close and its arrival brought most outdoor work to a halt. They were forced to rely on their wives and brothers to complete the work in the fields and to organize the grinding of barley grain for winter consumption. The nuns were working against the same climatic restrictions. They, like the villagers, used a water-powered grinder, operative only while the river and irrigation channels were still flowing. Once they froze, usually in late October, grinding could not be resumed until the thaw in the following May or June.

Every two or three days I left sorting the apricot stones until midday and spent the morning washing barley grain with the nuns in a small stream which ran in front of Julichang. Chuski and Samsten created a pool by damming and diverting the water until only a trickle could enter or leave. This drew off the chaff and other impurities which floated to the surface, leaving the heavier grain at the bottom of the pool. Tsultim brought bags of grain from the storerooms and slowly emptied their contents into the stream. Three of us crouched down uncomfortably on the stony path and, leaning over with our arms immersed to the elbow in icy water, we swirled the grain around to loosen the impurities. After about half an hour, the trickle of water leaving the pool began to run clear. With numbed hands, we clumsily heaped the sodden grain into a wicker basket on the bank and carried the heavy, wet barley into the courtyard. We washed only as much as could be spread out for drying. Throughout the day and the one after, we took it in turns to rake and turn the grain, exposing it to the few hours of intense heat from the midday sun. Later, Samsten roasted the grain.

This was carried out in one of the small rooms off the court-yard. I would hear the crackling and spitting of the fire and slowly the smell of roasted barley would seep into the air. Sometimes Samsten called me inside and gave me handfuls of hot, crunchy grain to eat. The heat was ferocious. I hovered by the open door, watching the flames of the fire cast different shadows and colours over the room. Samsten's face was streaked with soot and streams of perspiration ran like tears down her scorched cheeks; but all afternoon she sat there, toss-ing the grain over the hearth and spreading it thinly over wooden trays to cool. Once it had cooled it was carried down to the mill, a small stone hut situated in the woods below the nunnery and close to the river. Fast flowing water, directed along specially constructed channels, was harnessed to a heavy wooden paddle built beneath the hut; and the impact of the water was increased by diverting it, in the final stretch, down a narrow section of hollowed tree trunk so that it hit the blades of the paddle with great force, and their rotation turned the grinding stones in the hut above.

From the mill, the barley flour was taken to the nunnery's storerooms. Here, on most afternoons, I found the bursar hov-ering among the sacks, choosing how many to load on to the donkeys and transport to his own storerooms in the monas-tery. Tsultim spent most of her day going back and forth from the nunnery to the mill, carrying out grain and collecting up the newly ground flour. She was always caked in it. Tsultim was a well built woman, short and stocky with a handsome, rather squarish face; but by dusk her strong, straight shoulders had begun to sag. The work seemed relentless. Occasionally she put her head into the courtyard to ask for help; more often, though, we heard her comings and goings by the jangling sound of the large keys which hung from the sash at her waist. These she used to open the storerooms whenever the bursar came to inspect supplies. Time was now short. Soon the grind-ing device would have to be dismantled for the winter. The bursar watched Tsultim closely and he began to check daily the amounts of grain that were being ground.

The bursar was anxious, too, about the grain he expected from the *chomo* living at Lababs. It was mid-October and this grain had not yet arrived at the nunnery. Lababs, about an hour's walk from Julichang, was a small patch of irrigated land on a bank above the river and here two *chomo* grew barley for the monastery. These women were slow to finish their work because they could not rely on extra help and they themselves were no longer young and active. Everyone – monks, nuns, and villagers – seemed to have jokes to tell about the *chomo* of Lababs. Long before I met them I was acquainted with their eccentricities.

One afternoon I walked beyond the fork in the track, following the river for a couple of miles until I came across a cluster of trees which bordered terraced fields. The women were working outside. They were still winnowing and threshing the grain, tasks we had completed at Julichang weeks ago. I could see one of the *chomo* driving cattle, tethered to a central post, round and round over sheaves of barley which were spread across the floor of a small courtyard. This separated the grain from the stalks. The other *chomo* was tossing the chaff into piles and sweeping up the loose grain into sacks.

As they saw me approach, the two women stopped working and they shouted excitedly to me to cross the stepping stones in the river and climb the path to their compound. It was obvious that they rarely received visitors and were eager for news and contact. Although they knew I was living and working at Julichang, they tried their best to persuade me to stay with them at Lababs. Looking at them from close quarters, I understood how stories had grown up around them. Both women resembled a heap of rags. Their faces were weathered and stained black by a mixture of grime and wood smoke; their clothes were threadbare scraps of cloth, and they went about barefoot. One of them seemed completely deaf. The other chattered away at the top of her voice as if she had not spoken to anyone for weeks.

The *chomo* rested from their work for a while and we sat together by the ramshackle collection of whitewashed buildings where they lived. One of the women disappeared inside, returning a moment later with a pitcher of yoghurt and a pot of tea. The yoghurt was quite the best I had tasted in Ladakh; the tea, oily, greenish and rancid, among the worst. They raised some crops and kept a small herd of animals for Rizong and, like everyone else it seemed, they grumbled a lot about the bursar. The women also knew the limitations of their technology. The deaf one nodded and chuckled as the other asked me about electricity, light bulbs and television sets. They had heard about them and were fascinated by what such modern devices would mean for their own work. The *chomo* of Lababs were undoubtedly quirky, but I liked them. I continued to meet them from time to time, either on the footpath or at the nunnery. Occasionally one of them came to Julichang to collect supplies of tea and salt; and she would invariably try and tempt me with promises of unlimited yoghurt if I returned to live with the *chomo* at Lababs.

Four

There was an air of excitement at Julichang. From early morning the nuns were busy, sweeping and tidying the courtyard in anticipation of the arrival of a party of monks from Rizong. I wasn't sure what was happening, but Sonam told me to be ready in the kitchen. At any moment the bursar would arrive and I would be expected to help him prepare quantities of food.

The day, I learned, had been set aside for dyeing cloth. Long, narrow strips of woollen cloth were woven at the nunnery in April or May. They were rolled up and hung in the courtyard until the autumn, when they were dyed. Later, during the winter months, the monks and nuns would sew the strips into new monastic robes.

I had just finished reading through Sonam's scriptures when the first party arrived from the monastery. Ahead came the very young monks, boys six or seven years old, who bounded excitedly into the kitchen; behind followed several slightly older ones, the novices and the bursar. They unloaded their bags of rice and different spices which we would cook for lunch and I was put to work peeling the vegetables dug that morning from the nunnery garden. The boys quickly disappeared again, heading out into the sunshine with the bursar to begin building wood fires on the slopes above Julichang. Intrigued by the excited shouts and laughter which carried up to the kitchen, I peeped through the windows and saw Tsultim scouring huge iron pots in the stream below and a succession of monks and nuns carrying water to the dyeing area.

We were all waiting, however, for the arrival of Memi Nasten, the acting abbot of Rizong. His presence at the nunnery, with one or two other senior monks, marked the day as an important occasion. But it soon became obvious that it wasn't to be a solemn religious affair; rather, the whole day was marked by a picnic air with lots of food, noise and good humour. I recognized the signs that warned of Memi Nasten's approach and the flurry of activity which greeted his entrance to the nunnery. Everyone jumped to attention, bowing low as he swept in and we watched him quietly as he settled himself with his texts and prepared to make the offerings which inaugurated the day's work. On the orders of the bursar, I hurried out from the kitchen to serve Memi Nasten a pot of freshly made tea. I was always nervous in his presence, partly because I was still unsure of the language and afraid I would offend him by my clumsy expressions. Also I had an impression that he regarded me with some ambivalence. I was sensitive to being perceived as an intruder, an unwelcome visitor; and Memi Nasten's cool, almost disdainful air did nothing to allay these fears.

Work began in earnest. The abbot was responsible for weighing the dye. He measured out different quantities with careful accuracy and weighed them using a pair of the bursar's heavy brass scales. Some of the dye was commercially produced and had been brought from India; the rest was made from berries and certain kinds of tree bark. Only the day before, I had seen Tsultim and Samsten sharing the task of crushing the natural substances. They had used a great wooden pestle against a hollowed-out stone, hammering away until they created a powder which dissolved as the water was heated in the cauldrons.

The monks and nuns tended the wood fires, poking at the sticks and tossing lengths of cloth into the boiling dye, while the boys scurried between the kitchen and hillside with regular supplies of tea. The bursar had taken over the kitchen from Sonam and was issuing instructions in a jovial, friendly way; but, at the same time, we knew he was keeping a close eye on us to ensure that we weren't slacking. Sonam, disoriented by being ousted from the hearth, crouched in a corner. I glanced over to her as she sat glum and silent, sifting through a tray of rice; but from time to time when she looked up, I saw a familiar gleam in her eye and a half suppressed, complicit smile as we both watched the bursar bustling about the kitchen.

Absorbed as we were in the food preparations for the twenty or so workers at Julichang, we hardly noticed the morning vanish; but, at last we rested, joining everyone outside to eat a meal of rice and spiced vegetables. For the nuns and me it was a welcome respite from the usual heavy porridge and radish. After lunch the abbot returned to Rizong and the atmosphere became more relaxed. Some of the younger monks played pranks, splashing about in the stream; the boys became even more mischievous and made faces behind the bursar's back. Strips of cloth, stretched out to dry, covered the slopes above the nunnery; at the end of the afternoon, we rolled them up and the boys carried them back up the mountainside to Rizong.

The dyeing of cloth was followed, some days after, by the final work picnic of the year. The nuns told me that we were again expected to work with the abbot and monks; and on this occasion we would be clearing the vegetable fields before the frosts came. Sonam warned, though, that the work was exhausting and back-breaking. We would spend the day bent double, pulling vegetables from the ground.

Before the picnic the bursar was busy recruiting additional labour from Lababs and securing the help of another *chomo* who lived at Ule Tokpo, a nearby settlement. I was surprised when I learned later that this woman was the bursar's sister. The contrast in their appearance and circumstances could not have been more marked. He controlled a vast amount of wealth, much of it derived from our work and from that of the villagers; but his sister, always ragged and dirty, scratched a living as best she could on a small patch of land with a couple of cows. Any surplus she raised was given to the monastery and she was frequently called upon to assist the nuns in their work.

Early on I was puzzled by the fact that the nuns seemed to know exactly when the seasons would change. They even talked about the day they expected the first frost. On the morning of the picnic the sky was grey and overcast and the sun did not penetrate the heavy clouds. I felt, for the first time, that winter was near; but I was not prepared for the sharpness of the transition. Autumn became winter almost overnight.

The coolness in the air relieved some of the strain of working in the vegetable fields. Nevertheless, at the end of the day, I was thoroughly tired and every part of my body ached. We had begun soon after dawn. The bursar appeared early at Julichang and shooed us out to work shortly after our breakfast soup, organizing us into a line across the field. The *chomo* from Lababs and Ule Tokpo joined us and we started working our way slowly along the furrows. We pulled turnips, potatoes and carrots from the dry earth and threw them into the wicker baskets placed at different points in the field. We had already been working for an hour or so when Memi Nasten and a group of monks arrived from Rizong. By this time the boys had a good fire burning under the trees and they were making tea for the day. We were able to take a moment's rest when the first pot was served, but from then on we only snatched occasional breaks from work before lunch.

The monks were bound by the central Buddhist precept of non-violence. This meant that they could not work with us in clearing the ground for fear of killing insects in the soil. It did not prevent them, however, from sorting and cleaning the picked vegetables. As we filled the baskets, one of the young monks collected them and carried them over to where the monks sat. Their main task was to divide the vegetables into different piles according to their size and quality.

Again Sonam lost her kitchen to the bursar. Leaving us under the supervision of the monks, he disappeared to Julichang for most of the morning where, with help from the boys, he prepared a meal which was brought to us in the fields. We – the nuns, *chomo* and I – were so exhausted that we were virtually silent during lunch, but the monks kept up a lively chatter. After all, their work had been far less taxing, while we felt pushed to the limits of our strength. It took a real effort of will to resume vegetable picking after the meal as, during the brief rest from work, our limbs had become stiff and sore.

By mid-afternoon most of the field had been cleared and the old monk in charge of the monastery's donkeys had arrived with five animals to transport the produce to Rizong. In the autumn he spent almost every day going up and down the mountain path with heavily laden donkeys. He seemed to have had some kind of stroke as he was partly paralysed on one side of his body and had difficulty speaking. He was embarrassed by his clumsiness and he did not take much part in the religious life of the monastery; but because he was still physically strong, the bursar made him responsible for much of the drudgery. On many days he ate lunch with us at Julichang. I noticed that the nuns were very kind to him. In their dealings with him they were not so constrained by the reserve expected by more learned monks and they shared a very similar work load.

The bursar supervised the loading of the donkeys, strapping the full sacks of vegetables to their backs. It took several journeys between the fields and Rizong before all the produce was transferred to the bursar's storerooms. The smallest and poorest-quality vegetables were left behind for us.

After the monks had returned to Rizong, Sonam and I scoured the fields for any remaining vegetables. It was a furtive operation and Sonam told me to say nothing about it to the bursar. It would mean that for a few weeks more we could enjoy vegetables in our soup at the nunnery. By scrabbling under the dry earth we were able to find quite a number of potatoes, carrots and turnips which had been missed during the day's work. We hid them in our skirts in case we met any monks on the path and carried them back to Julichang. We made three or four trips to the fields before dusk settled and it became impossible for us to search any further. Sonam buried the vegetables in a pile of soil at the back of the kitchen. Here they would be protected from frost and hidden from the sharp eye of the bursar.

For days after the vegetable picking, the nuns, no strangers to hard graft, were still complaining that their bodies were stiff and aching. Gradually, though, I felt the pace of work beginning to slacken and the women prepared to change over from the summer to the winter tasks. Urgen left for the monastery and the courtyard was cleared in anticipation of snow. It could arrive at any time.

I helped Sonam move from the light, airy kitchen which we had been using over the last few months. Being situated at the top of the nunnery it was usually the first place to receive sunshine in the morning; for some days now it had remained in shadow for the whole day and a chilly draught blew through the wooden shutters. We spent a morning transferring the cooking pots and utensils to the winter quarters, a dingy windowless room tucked away in the lower levels and close to the nunnery's entrance.

One important task remained before the severe cold set in. This was the preservation of a portion of the vegetables sent down from the monastery by the bursar. It was chiefly the responsibility of Sonam. She cooked the vegetables, but most of us helped to spice, oil and press them into large iron pots. There was an air of secrecy about the work. The nuns did not want the bursar to see exactly how much had been preserved as they hoped to keep some for themselves, to supplement the plain monotony of the winter diet. We all agreed to be party to the conspiracy and later enjoyed dips into the pot we had kept behind.

Part Two
The Coming of Winter

Five

There was a strange silence to the morning when I awoke. For a moment I was disoriented until I realized that snow had fallen overnight, muffling the familiar sounds from the river. Only a week earlier we had moved to the winter kitchen and I had stopped sleeping outside, on the roof of Julichang. Now my belongings and blankets were stored indoors and at night I bedded down in the abandoned summer kitchen.

The cold was intense. I found that the hardest thing was to get up in the morning, to leave the warmth of my sleeping bag and emerge into the bitter air. Once dawn broke and I heard the nuns moving about below, I steeled myself to jump out and, throwing my heavy coat over my shoulders, I ran shivering down to the kitchen where Sonam was stoking the fire. I had on as many clothes as I possessed – layers of vests, woollen stockings, trousers and pullovers. I wore them in the day and slept in them at night. The only layer I removed when I went to bed was a thick Ladakhi overcoat. It was, like everything else, stained black from the fire and it carried a pungent odour of wood smoke. The smell and the grime from the fire were also ingrained on every exposed inch of my body.

To my horror, I discovered that the warm layers of clothes provided a comfortable home for fleas. Sometimes my whole body felt as if it was moving, a sensation I could not have imagined until I had experienced it. But I was not alone. All the other nuns had fleas. We used to huddle together around the smoky fire and we amused ourselves turning back the seams of our clothes so we could pluck these guests from their snug resting places. Although matters became worse during the winter, particularly when we worked in a tiny room surrounded by piles of fleeces, I learned like everyone else to resign myself to the fleas. It wasn't easy, but there really was no choice. Periodically and with great glee, the nuns pointed out the minute ticks which jumped across the floor, heading I knew, straight for our warm bodies. It was impossible to be unaware of them as they burrowed into the seams of our clothes and tormented us with a hundred pinpricks which scratching failed to relieve.

We could not wash properly. In order to bring water from the river, Sonam had to break through several inches of ice. Beneath it the water was still flowing, but it often froze as soon as she scooped it out. Before breakfast she heated a small amount for washing. Fuel was scarce and the water was never hot. There was just enough for all of us to splash our hands and faces before rubbing butter into our skin for protection against the biting wind. It was the same with washing clothes – the routine, everyday tasks suddenly seemed difficult and cumbersome. Unless it had been warmed, you could not put your hands in the icy water; and garments took forever to dry. I once made the mistake of trying to wash a pair of socks in the river. I dipped them into the water through the hole in the ice made by Sonam. The moment I lifted them out, they froze into solid lumps of ice which I had to keep by the fire for days before they thawed and dried out.

In the early weeks of the winter there was only a sprinkling of snow on the ground. Often the clouds were heavy and threatening, but when they hung low in the sky they took the edge off the piercing cold of a clear day. Julichang was in shadow. For over a month the sun's rays did not reach down into the narrow valley which housed the nunnery. By contrast the monastery, situated at a higher altitude, continued to receive many hours of sunlight during this period. I used to look forward to climbing the mountain path in the afternoon to retrieve the cattle since I could rest in the bright sunshine and enjoy the infusion of warmth as the chill lifted from my body for the first time in the day.

At the nunnery we tried to keep warm by crouching over a wood fire lit in the room where we worked in daylight hours. The smoke was acrid. It made our eyes smart and throats dry, but the fire was the only source of heat and just a few feet away from it the air felt bitterly cold. Sometimes, looking across the hearth at Damchos and Tsering I wondered how they would survive the winter. Damchos was the oldest nun at Julichang.

She was frail and blind and her wasted body was a poignant reminder of the harshness of Himalayan life. Tsering, too, had not been spared its cruelty, her face haggard and prematurely aged with years of suffering from severe arthritic pain. I felt almost guilty when I thought of my own fears of a Ladakhi winter; but I knew I was going to be tested by the harsh conditions. The last winter in Dharmsala had not been easy and I felt apprehensive. This time the place was much more remote and isolated. It was impossible for me to leave Ladakh in the depths of winter. The road into Kashmir was closed until the spring, sometimes the passes were not clear until as late as June, and the weekly flight from Leh was erratic. As long as my health held, I thought I would probably manage. I had learned in the miserable damp winter of the previous year that it was minor illnesses which brought on terrible depression. When I was ill, I dreamed of material comforts, especially warm beds and long, luxurious baths, and I tried to shut out the frustrations and doubts which crowded in. At these times, trying to penetrate the language and to adjust to a new and strange society seemed an impossible task.

But it was in the grey, cold weeks of the Ladakhi winter that I really drew close to the nuns. I had worked alongside them in most of their autumn tasks and I now felt caught up in the affairs of the community. Nevertheless, without being fully conscious of it, I still perceived these women through the eyes of the monastery. All my reading about Buddhism and my experiences in Dharmsala had reinforced a perspective which placed nuns at the margins of spiritual life. They were regarded as uneducated in the Buddhist scriptures and incapable of undertaking esoteric meditative practices.

Day after day, as winter closed in around us, we sat together talking and gossiping while we carded and spun wool. I began to see the nuns differently. It was partly because I shared their life, a kind of life I had not expected; and it forced me to ask myself certain simple questions. What did all this work for the monastery mean? Why didn't the nuns complain or show any obvious dissatisfaction with their lot? If we had no time to study or meditate, why distinguish ourselves from village women? The answers were not immediately obvious; but I continued to seek them and, in seeking them, I began to throw off many of the preconceptions with which I was encumbered.

The sharp transition from autumn to winter was accompanied by changes at Rizong. Monks returned from trading in distant places, and a stream of pilgrims began to arrive as they made their way around Ladakh's monasteries. In the months when cultivation and outdoor work were impossible, Ladakhis took the opportunity to earn merit, to fulfil religious obligations. Most villagers merely spent more time on observances at home; they read texts, recited prayers, counted rosary beads and visited the monks to invite them to perform household ceremonies. A number left the village and travelled between different monasteries for up to four or five months. They attended religious festivals and received hospitality from the monks and nuns of the different communities.

The pilgrimage to the Buddhist shrines in India, however, was the journey of a lifetime. For monks and nuns in particular, it was something most hoped to undertake at least once.

Chuski was preparing for her pilgrimage to India. She had been saving tiny amounts of money for years, gifts from relatives and visitors to the nunnery until, at last, she could afford to go. With a small party of monks and villagers she was planning to catch the last bus into Kashmir before the mountain passes closed.

First of all the pilgrims were to visit Dharmsala, the home of the Dalai Lama. From there they would travel to Varanasi and Bohdgaya, the places associated with the birth, teaching and Enlightenment of Gautama, the historical Buddha. Finally, they intended to make their way to Mungod in southern India where Rizong's abbots resided. Chuski and her party were not expected to return to Ladakh until the spring.

Shortly before Chuski was to depart, her travelling companion arrived at Julichang from Leh. Chodel, a nun, was a tall ungainly woman who immediately shattered the calm of nunnery life with her shrill non-stop chatter. One of the nuns took me aside and warned me of her "peculiarities". I didn't know quite what she meant, but Chodel told terrific stories. She held us all spellbound with her gossip and intrigue, mixing fact and fiction in uncertain proportions. Sonam hinted strongly at marital scandals in her past; but the nuns were prepared to treat her with considerable deference. She was the sister of one of Ladakh's highest-ranking lamas and was rumoured to have immense wealth. It did not go unnoticed by us that the bursar was careful to be attentive to her needs.

Chuski and Chodel were excited and nervous about the journey ahead. It dominated their conversation and they pestered for advice the one or two nuns who had already made the pilgrimage. India was feared as a vast and foreign country. They were warned to be on their guard against bad food and water, losing their money, and being cheated by unscrupulous strangers. The rules were different in India and the women should not assume anything.

The morning of their departure finally came. We pressed sums of money into their hands and the nuns promised to take offerings for us at the different shrines. I stood with Sonam, Samsten and Tsultim at the entrance to Julichang and we watched them as they disappeared down the path to the main road, carrying their bulky bed rolls and a few belongings. We half-envied them the prospect of adventure; but, at the same time, we were secretly relieved to be staying behind in the security of the monastic routine.

Suddenly Julichang seemed quiet and empty; but not for long. Namgyal Stonchok, a celebration of the Buddha's descent from the heavenly realms, inaugurated the winter cycle of religious festivals and was shortly to be celebrated at Rizong. The monastery observed a liturgical calendar based upon the key events in the Buddha's life and, in addition, several auspicious days relating to the history of the religion in Tibet were woven into the sequence of rituals.

Rizong, rather than the nunnery, now became the focus of activity; preparations for the ceremony were already underway. As usual the bursar was active in his attempts to persuade us to spend our afternoons at the monastery; and I often joined Samsten and Tsultim in Rizong's kitchen, helping to scrub the cooking pots and to peel the great quantities of vegetables which would feed the monks and villagers attending the festival.

There were many unfamiliar faces at Rizong, monks who had been away supervising the harvest in various villages or trading goods in remote areas of Changthang, Nubra, and Zanskar. They were surprised to learn that I was living at Julichang and they rarely hid their amusement when I explained my interest in the life of nuns. I had become used to this response, but I was irritated by it. I would think about how hard the nuns worked to support the monastery and yet they continued to be denied any recognition or status. My own body ached through hours of tedious manual work. Although I resigned myself to the routine of work, there were many occasions when I bit my tongue as I struggled to show the deference expected by the monks.

During the autumn, groups of monks from Rizong had frequently called at Julichang, and one or two were willing to help me study Sonam's scriptures. They would go over the texts with me, correcting my pronunciation and explaining the meaning of certain passages. I often found it difficult to keep up with them, but I persevered because I thought it was the key to understanding the religious life and I believed that the texts and their custodians, the monks, were the backbone of the Buddhist tradition.

At the same time I was conscious of the fact that some of the monks I knew did not seem to have any spiritual persona at all. The more I thought about it the more I realized that there was no particular reason why they should. The majority had been given to the monastery by their parents as young boys. They passed through the formal two-stage admission: novicehood (the acceptance of five Buddhist precepts – not to kill, steal, live unchastely, lie, or consume alcohol) and full ordination (the acceptance of a further five precepts – not to eat after midday, not to partake in dancing and music, not to adorn the body with flowers or perfume, not to use high seats, and not to receive gold or silver). Many boys were trained in the scriptures and schooled in the ways of monastic life without necessarily having any natural inclination towards them. I was becoming wary of notions of spirituality, mysticism and holy men. Perhaps it was because I was a woman or because I was an outsider struggling with a strange language, but I was conscious of a tension, a disparity between my expectations of monks and how they actually appeared to me. Most were just ordinary men doing a job, a number were friendly and amusing, a few even loud and boorish. There were, of course, notable exceptions. Achok Rinpoche was one. Soon I was to meet another.

Achok was my first teacher, and he became my guide through the maze of texts, rituals and symbols which made up

Tibetan Buddhism. I had met him by chance in Dharmsala the year before, and my early impressions were of a tall, slender and rather dignified young man. His face and head, however, struck me as rather unusual. He had prominent cheekbones which gave his face an angular appearance; his skin was smooth and taut, almost flawless but for a group of dark moles on his chin. Achok's head, like that of all monks, was closely shaven and the absence of hair revealed its distinctive pointed shape. He explained to me later that this feature and the facial marks had been critical in the discovery that he was the incarnation of a distinguished Gelugpa lama.

At the age of three Achok became abbot of a group of monasteries in eastern Tibet. Although as a *rinpoche* or precious one, he held special status, he was not exempt from the rigorous tests and examinations required of all monks as they passed through the different stages of monastic ordination. Under the guidance of his tutors and guardians, Achok was taught to read and write in the monastery; he was instructed in matters of doctrine and philosophy; he memorized hundreds of texts; he became skilled in forms of public debate; and he developed techniques of meditation. Above all, his accumulation of Buddhist knowledge or wisdom went hand in hand with his penetration of the secrets of spiritual practice. His understanding of the path to salvation was subtle and profound. For him to read and understand a text was one thing, but to contemplate it, to "realize" it, was something else. This was the struggle of his vocation.

Achok was deeply immersed in the spiritual life, he knew no other one; but despite the many years of monastic seclusion, he was not an austere, monkish figure. I found him gentle and compassionate, aware of the contradictions and complexity of the human condition. Often in conversation he admitted doubt or uncertainty on matters of Buddhist doctrine and practice; but he always refused to retreat into scholasticism, dogma or orthodoxy.

Among the monks returning to Rizong in the late autumn was Rigdol. Sonam had already spoken to me about him. He was abbot of Julichang with overall responsibility for the affairs of the nunnery. The bursar may have been more visible, but his role was confined to organizing work and did not include the institution of female devotees as such; sometimes, though, I found it difficult to imagine that there was any difference between the two.

A couple of days prior to the festival, Rigdol arrived at Julichang. He was tired after a long journey by horse and on foot from Zanskar. He rested before making the steep ascent to Rizong, and he asked Sonam to bring me to the kitchen when he heard from the nuns that I had been living with them for many weeks. He wanted to know more about where I had come from and what I was doing in the nunnery.

I stood awkwardly before Rigdol, conscious of my grimy dishevelled appearance. But he motioned for me to sit near him and take tea. I was immediately drawn to him. He was much respected as a Buddhist scholar; but, like Achok, he seemed to combine his scriptural knowledge with a sensitivity I rarely encountered among monks. Although Rigdol was in late middle age, there was no hint of coarseness in his features. His face was refined; but, as I looked more carefully, I saw the wear of many years of study and meditation. His eyes were clear and steady; and watching me closely, he listened, occasionally interrupting or encouraging me as I stumbled to explain myself. He was interested to know if I could read the scriptures, and when he learned I could, he invited me to study with him in the afternoons at Rizong. I was thrilled. Sonam hurried to tell the other nuns and they were pleased too. Often when I returned from Rizong, Tsering would call me to the workroom where she spent the day turning the pages of her scriptures and counting rosary beads with her swollen arthritic hands. She was anxious to help me improve my reading and to advise me about how I should behave in the presence of learned monks. Everyone at Julichang thought it was a great opportunity for me to receive proper instruction in the Buddhist doctrines. Already I had noted the mixture of warmth and deference with which the women approached Rigdol; it was not something I often observed in their relations with other Rizong monks. For me, the meeting with Rigdol left a feeling which was new: the desire to be in his presence for no other reason than that this man emanated calm and equanimity.

Six

I hardly slept the night before Namgyal Stonchok. I was anxious about the two days of ceremony to be held at Rizong. I still remembered my first day-long temple ceremony for the excruciating stiffness in my limbs, for the bewildering array of offerings which filled the altars, and for the extraordinary and dissonant sounds which interrupted the smooth, almost hypnotic, scriptural recitation. I learned, too, what it meant when I had read in books that the Tibetan pantheon was crowded with gods, deities, spirits and all kinds of supernatural beings, some ferocious, others benign. It seemed confusing, and almost impossible to find a way through the complex symbolism and ritual enacted in the temple. Then I had relied heavily on Achok's guidance. Now, several times a week, I received instruction from Rigdol; he introduced me to a number of Buddhist texts and explained aspects of ceremonial and meditative practice.

I had always sensed that the power and authority of monks did not depend on their fluency in the scriptures. Rather it derived from their ability to go beyond what was written in the texts and to harness their learning to a set of secret ritual practices. Young boys admitted to Rizong as novices, the first rung of the monastic hierarchy, were placed under the supervision of a senior monk. He was responsible for teaching the philosophy of Mahayana Buddhism and the importance of discipline; but he also prepared his pupils for initiation. The relationship between master and pupil was fundamental. It was the key to the penetration of Tibetan Buddhism. Only after many years of instruction and initiation at the hands of a spiritual guide could monks "realize" the doctrine. This meant that they had moved beyond the text. They left behind, temporarily, the limitations of this world to participate directly in esoteric realms of infinite power. The attainment of this state was the objective of meditation and of occasions of temple ceremony. Critical in the ability to act as a medium was the celibate body. Celibacy was a means for the concentration of power. Women could never assume this role; their bodies were deemed weak, impure and unsuitable for ritual manipulation.

This became clear to me during the winter cycle of religious ceremonies when I found myself, along with the nuns, confined to the margins of whatever was happening inside Rizong's temple. Sometimes we were not admitted to the temple at all and we spent our day in the kitchen below, with the sound of the monks' chanting in our ears as a constant reminder of our exclusion from spiritual practice. At first these experiences were mixed up with my fears of being an outsider; and I tended to be preoccupied with my acceptance into the life of Julichang. The ambivalence of Memi Nasten still bothered me and I thought, rather resentfully, that while he was probably happy to have me working in the nunnery, he was suspicious of my presence at Rizong. Having discovered many months before that I could not sustain the anthropologist role I had set out with, I learned, rather painfully, that giving it up had left me exposed and vulnerable in my relations with people. Perceived slights and misunderstandings weighed heavily and I found it difficult to shake them off.

But increasingly I concentrated on my experience of being a *chomo*. It seemed to contain within itself all the historical ambiguities which surrounded the status of women in Buddhism. I seemed to be able to adapt myself easily to a role which was, in effect, an inversion of the place I occupied in my own society. From being an educated person of high status, I had become a domestic drudge. Yet becoming a *chomo* did not involve any deception on my part. I did not have to pretend to be Buddhist or that I had any intention of entering a monastic order. I was a *chomo* simply because I was a single woman living as part of a community of nuns and bound by the precepts of female monastic life. The nuns accepted me as such and did not demand more.

Namgyal Stonchok was going to be my first real encounter with Rizong as a spiritual community. I approached the ceremony with mixed feelings. Until now I had seen the monks almost exclusively in their role as representatives of a powerful and worldly monastic empire – as traders, brokers, supervisors of work. I hoped that as a result of Rigdol's instruction I would be more aware of what went on in the temple, but I didn't quite know what to expect.

The nuns rose early and hurried to complete the morning's tasks before leaving for Rizong. From daybreak, parties of travellers began to arrive at the nunnery; these were pious lay men and women, some from nearby villages, others from afar. They were on their way to the monastery for the ceremony, but as they approached Julichang, Tsodpah called them inside for refreshments. Bringing fresh tea from the kitchen to serve to the visitors, I passed Tsultim, bundled up against the cold as she opened the nunnery storerooms with her great iron keys and took out extra supplies of flour and dried fruit to offer to the pilgrims. The nuns enjoyed few such luxuries themselves; but they shared what they had with anyone who called at Julichang. Offering hospitality, Sonam once explained to me, was a way of earning merit and, during the winter months in particular, a good deal was accumulated by the nuns.

We set out along the path to the monastery. The solid, bulky figures of Tsultim and Tsodpah strode ahead. Behind followed the tall, slender Samsten, her pale cheeks flushed against the cold; then came Sonam who, freed from her kitchen for the day excitedly bounded along. Watching how much work she had already done since first light, it was hard for me, struggling as I was to keep up with her, to know where she found the energy. The morning was bitterly cold and occasional flurries of fine snow fell from the sky. Two of the older nuns, Damchos and Tsering, remained behind. We left them with a well-stoked fire and a large pot of tea. They did not expect us to return until the late afternoon. The ceremony in Rizong's temple had started before dawn, and as we approached the final ascent we heard the low, continuous rhythm of recitation. It was punctuated by violent crescendos of drums, trumpets, horns, bells, and cymbals. The monastery was alive with activity. Streams of pilgrims wound their way around the different buildings and many clustered outside the main temple, prostrating themselves at its entrance. None, however, dared cross the threshold.

The bursar was under siege. He was trying to supervise the preparations for tea and lunch as well as guard his storerooms from the intrusion of inquisitive visitors. He was clearly relieved to see the nuns arrive and he directed us straight to the kitchen, where the boys were working at full stretch. It took a few moments before my eyes adjusted to the dim light and dense smoke of the kitchen. Over the floor were scattered iron pots, bags of flour and rice, and baskets overflowing with vegetables. The novices were scurrying up and down the steep, uneven steps with supplies of fresh tea. There was no time for their usual boyish jokes and pranks and they feared the wrath of the senior monks in the temple. Namgyal Stonchok was not an occasion for playful, juvenile subversion.

The nuns took charge in their quiet, efficient way. They set to work stoking the fire, churning tea and sifting the rice and flour. Gradually, the frenetic pace of work relaxed into a comfortable routine and the bursar retreated into his rooms, confident that he had taken things in hand.

I escaped from the thick, smoky atmosphere and carried the baskets of vegetables on to the bursar's verandah for sorting and peeling. It was a monotonous, seemingly endless task and it gave me plenty of time to regret that I had ever revealed my possession of a sharp Swiss army knife. Although I was glad to be working outdoors, I was frequently forced to stop, to warm my fingers and revive my cold, cramped limbs. I was conscious of being scrutinized by curious villagers, who were surprised to find a young Englishwoman working with the nuns at Rizong; but the bursar was protective of both me and his storerooms and he kept onlookers at a safe distance. He was concerned, too, that I should not be distracted from my task, as the vegetables were to be the mainstay of the lunch.

The noise and commotion surrounding the work in the kitchen did not impinge on what was happening inside the temple. The concentration of the monks, summoned before daybreak by the long, haunting call of monastic trumpets, was intense. They were moving slowly through the different stages of a spiritual journey towards the climax. Here they would, for a moment, enter realms of great mystical power. I knew the temple had been carefully prepared over many days for the ceremony, for each afternoon, when I collected the cattle from Rizong, I had seen the younger monks sweeping and cleaning, and beating dust from the faded silks which hung on the walls of the temple. Hundreds of butter lamps were polished and made ready for offering on the altars to Chenresig, the male deity incarnated in the Dalai Lama and the embodiment of compassion and mercy; to Dolma, his female consort, the saviour or deliverer; and to Tsongkhapa, the great reformer of Buddhism in Tibet and founder of the Gelugpa school. However, these were not to be the main focus of the ceremony. A specially constructed mandala, over six feet high, dominated the temple interior. The mandala was a wooden pyramidal structure built by the senior monks. It had a series of steps, leading to the pinnacle on which offerings were arranged to arouse the five senses. The mandala symbolized the spiritual journey, the unfolding religious experience; its realization involved movement from the periphery to the inner core, and simultaneously, movement from the lower levels of the mandala to its apex. It was a contemplative exercise undertaken individually by the monks and collectively by them as a community.

The monks remained undisturbed in their ritual practices throughout the morning. Outside we were only aware of the shifts in the rhythm of their recitation and the sudden bursts of sound from the trumpets, drums, cymbals and bells. We could not know what was happening inside the temple. The bursar hurried us in our preparations for lunch. He told us that the monks would break at midday and then we would be allowed to enter the temple briefly with the lay men and women.

One moment it seemed I was being pleasantly lulled into daydreaming by the tedium of my work and the regular rise and fall of the monk's voices; the next moment I was aware that the noise had ceased. Monks began to appear at the entrance of the temple, shielding their eyes as they adjusted to the glare of the day and stretching their stiffened bodies. They had been hunched beneath their heavy robes, sitting cross-legged in the dim glow of the butter lamps since well before dawn. Such concentration required considerable physical stamina.

The villagers slowly filed into the temple. They stooped low, a shuffling collection of men, women and children, anxious to bring themselves into contact with the sacred objects. They moved between the different altars, touching each with their foreheads and mumbling prayers and mantras. The nuns followed. I was taken aback by my first glimpse of the temple. Inside we could hardly move for the mass of ritual paraphernalia – altars, offerings, butter lamps, dough effigies, scriptures, musical instruments, robes – strewn untidily across the floor. The temple resembled a work place and, in a sense, that was its function.

The monks did not give us much time and soon they were preparing to take up their places again. The nuns and I hastened to return to the kitchen where the lunch was being ladled out on to a stack of tin plates. The boys served the abbot and senior monks first of all and I helped the nuns carry the remaining plates, piled high with food, into the temple. We sat down to eat with the monks, but the villagers crouched near the door. They were ill at ease and barely touched the food, preferring to empty the rice and vegetables into large grubby handkerchiefs which they pushed down the front pouches of their overcoats. Later they shared out and enjoyed these luxuries. But what they were really waiting for, with growing impatience, was the distribution of the gods' food. I was surprised by the strange mixture of reverence and boredom shown by the villagers. Their restlessness continued to grow, until their chatter forced Memi Nasten to call for the large dough effigy to be brought to him. It had been offered to the benign deities and spirits earlier in the morning and was imbued with their blessings. Accompanied by an almost deafening cacophony of sound from all the musical instruments played at once, the abbot reaffirmed the effigy's purity. He ordered the junior monks to break the dough into pieces and dispense it to everyone present. Like much of the food served before, the dough pieces went straight into the front pouches of our coats, nestling against all kinds of stale scraps. The villagers scrambled to their feet first, relieved at last to be dismissed from the temple. It was the cue for our departure. I helped the nuns gather up the half-eaten plates of food from the monks and we returned to the kitchen. The monks closed the heavy temple doors on the noise and distraction of the outside world; and we found ourselves shut out, once more, from the magical time and space created in Buddhist ceremony.

It was still early afternoon, but the sky was dark and overcast. The sun had not broken through the thick layer of cloud and the threat of snow hung heavily in the air. Sonam pointed out to me a group of eagles, wheeling and circling high above the mountain ridge. I had never seen such magnificent birds before, but the Ladakhis viewed them with ambivale.ice. They were an omen of winter.

Already, the villagers were starting to drift away from the monastery, content in the knowledge that they had earned valuable merit. Their attendance at Namgyal Stonchok was an auspicious beginning to the long, harsh season ahead. We finished our work in the kitchen, cleaning pots and plates, churning fresh tea. For us the day was virtually over. For the monks it would extend well beyond darkness. Following the track down through the dry valley we suddenly felt free, as the weight of respect and solemnity maintained throughout our visit to the monastery lifted. All the way back to Julichang, the nuns told stories, laughing and joking and exchanging the gossip they had picked up from the villagers. I was tired. It had turned out to be a different kind of day from the one I had imagined; and I wondered what the auspicious nature of the occasion would mean for me.

Seven

The monastery was eerily silent. There was no sign of the monks. Sonam had asked me to bring some kerosene and spices, and I was looking for the bursar. I threaded my way through the maze of cells and as I passed the kitchen, I caught sight of the boys playing. On hearing footsteps outside, they paused for a moment, fearful that the sound marked the arrival of one of the monks; but when they saw it was me they relaxed, and greeted me with cheeky grins stretched wide across their dirt-streaked faces. They were enjoying their release from the round of work which was usually carried out under the stern eye of one or two senior monks. The boys knew the bursar well enough to get away with certain tricks, tricks they never dared play with the others. The bursar ignored them and, in his long-suffering way, he took these minor rebellions to be just one of the burdens of the job.

The bursar told me that most of the monks had left for Yangthang, the village most closely associated with the monastery. They had gone to perform a cycle of household ceremonies which would last for twelve days. Its purpose was to ward off dangers, misfortune or sickness; and each occasion involved the reading of religious texts, accompanied by offerings and purification, in a different village house. The monks were responsible for the spiritual welfare of the villagers and, through these ceremonies, they went some way towards repaying the lay men and women for the produce and labour they supplied to the monastery.

I could see that the bursar was eager to take advantage of the monks' absence. He wanted to finish various tasks before they returned from Yangthang and he planned to enlist my help. His method was a simple one of flattery. He praised the efficiency with which I had worked through the apricot stones at Julichang and, brushing aside the evidence of the damage it had caused to my fingers, he directed me to a large pile heaped inside his storerooms. The nuns were amused when I told them I had been hired by the bursar for work at Rizong and they tried to cheer me up, telling me that I would be well fed and would have plenty of opportunities for persuading the bursar to part with luxuries, such as walnuts, sweet kernels or dried apricots.

At first it seemed strange to be at the monastery from early morning and I felt disorientated. The regime of work, so familiar to me from my earliest days in Ladakh, had changed and I was unsure of my place in a different set of tasks. I knew that the previous feeling of integration I experienced while living with the nuns had its roots in my ability to work closely with them, to shoulder some of the burden of their chores and to expose myself, without mediation, to the life they led. But I was always conscious of how precarious was the sense of belonging and now I feared its loss through my exclusion from the winter routine. I worried that I might find myself unwittingly an anthropologist again, becoming marginal and dependent, an onlooker who could not contribute to the community of women.

But working at the monastery did not turn out to be as bad as I had imagined, mainly because I was kept company by a party of men from Yangthang hired to paint the outside walls of Rizong's temples and monastic cells. The bursar was outnumbered and he knew he would have to keep us all in good humour if the work was to be completed in the short time available. He spent most of the morning supervising the boys in the kitchen and at midday we were served a generous lunch; but the bursar found it difficult to hide his impatience and he begrudged giving us the time we needed to eat the food. He tried to secure my co-operation by regularly passing me a handful of apricots or walnuts which I tucked into the pouch of my coat and later shared with the nuns. The village men were not so lucky. They were allowed, though, to drink beer after their day's work and, at dusk, I returned to Julichang with two or three of the villagers who collected fresh supplies of alcohol from Tsodpah. They carried the pots of beer back to the small guest-house below Rizong where the men slept. The beer washed down their supper, the cold leftovers from lunch, and insulated them against the freezing night air.

I knew several of the Yangthang men because I had met them at Julichang while they were transporting grain for the monastery in the weeks before Namgyal Stonchok. They introduced me to the others in the group. At first the villagers were unsure of me – I was a foreigner, a young woman living and working as a *chomo* at Julichang. It was puzzling to them and I was always conscious of their careful scrutiny as I went about my tasks. Eventually their curiosity got the better of them and they began to ask question after question. The men needed to place me by finding out about my parents, my brothers and sisters, my house, my past. Since my grasp of the language was still shaky, I often surprised them (and myself) with my answers to their queries. These idiosyncrasies provoked laughter in the village party and helped to overcome the initial reserve I sensed in the mens' association with me.

Slowly, I learned more about their own lives; and my being a *chomo* seemed to be an advantage in persuading the men to talk, particularly about marriage and family life. I discovered that most of them were part of polyandrous households – a set of brothers shared a single wife and they all worked together to raise crops on the pieces of land leased to them from the monastery. Usually it was only the eldest son who went through a formal wedding ceremony, acting on behalf of his younger brothers, and at marriage he took over the family house from his parents. As head of the household he became responsible for supplying the labour owed to the monastery and he took turns with his other brothers to work away from the village when their help was requested by the bursar. His father and mother were moved into a smaller dwelling nearby, sometimes attached to the family house as a kind of outhouse, and they were often accompanied by their unmarried daughters who cared for them in their old age. Most families could not afford more than one dowry, which was given to the eldest daughter when she married; the usual fate of a younger sister was to become a *chomo*, looking after her elderly parents and helping her brother's wife with the running of the household.

A wedding was an important event in the village and the men described to me the extensive preparations involved, the splendour of the costumes worn by the groom and his party, and the great feasting which everyone enjoyed over many days. Listening to their vivid descriptions I could imagine such scenes, but I found it almost impossible to conjure up in my mind any clear image of the bride. I had never seen the villagers' wives; they did not visit the nunnery and I had never met any at Rizong. I did not know why this should be so and the more I thought about it, the more curious it seemed.

Once the painting of the monastery buildings was completed, the men moved down the mountainside to undertake jobs around the nunnery. Although the size of the group remained the same, a number of the men returned to Yangthang and were replaced by their brothers. I sensed that the women looked forward to their arrival, since their presence at Julichang relieved the isolation of winter and the villagers were full of the usual local news and gossip. For many days beforehand Tsodpah, the nun in charge of the brewing of beer, was absent from the work being carried out by the fireside. Occasionally I caught sight of her, a stout figure with red glowing cheeks and a broad smile, as she emerged from one of the rooms whose entrance was hidden beneath the wooden ladder which led to the summer kitchen. Here she kept several pots of barley grain at different stages of fermentation and she took care to ensure that there was a good supply of beer to satisfy the villagers. It helped relieve some of the tension created by the bursar's presence at the nunnery for most of the day.

Later, when the bursar had returned to Rizong, we all gathered around the smoky fire which burned haphazardly in the winter workroom. The nuns, having taken formal Buddhist vows which admitted them to religious life at the lowest level as novices, were strict in their abstinence from alcohol; but Dondrup and I, being *chomo*, were permitted to share beer with the men. I noticed that, after a few bowls of alcohol, either Dondrup began to doze, her snores provoking amusement among the men, or she became talkative, even gay, shedding the scowling expression which her face carried for most of the day. I was cautious, though, having learned to my cost that the beer was deceptively potent. It never made me feel drunk; but I suffered terribly the next morning if I had too much.

In the evenings the nuns were not idle. They were busy cleaning, carding and spinning wool while the villagers, tired but jovial, looked on, peering through the smoke and darkness to sustain a lively exchange with us. The men were now very familiar to me and I felt pleased to be part of the gathering, to be able to tell my own stories about the bursar – how he had "persuaded" me to do this or that kind of work, what I had seen in his storerooms, and so on. The atmosphere in the workroom was lighthearted and everyone laughed at the different accounts, but I was conscious of a growing antagonism between the men and the bursar. I didn't understand yet how important the nuns were in mediating this difficult relationship between lay and monastic life.

During their first days at Julichang, a number of the village men were set to work on the outside of the nunnery buildings. They were high-spirited, sloshing thin white paint over the uneven mud walls and splattering each other by their reckless method. From inside, we could hear their voices echoing around the courtyard as they shouted to one another, dangling precariously with their cans of paint from rickety wooden ladders. The bursar, however, was out of earshot; he was with the rest of the party in the woods where heavy work was being done.

The dense clustering of trees, a rare sight in Ladakh, ran along the river bank between the nunnery and Lababs. The younger men, at the bursar's instigation, were climbing high into the trees; he stood below, shouting orders to them as they cautiously made their way along the stronger middle branches and began cutting into the dry, brittle wood. The older villagers waited for the heavy branches to fall. They dragged them away from the trees to a clearing, where they could be cut into smaller pieces, sorted into piles and loaded on to donkeys for transportation to Rizong. This was to be the monastery's supply of winter fuel.

Usually the Yangthang men departed for the woods in the early morning and did not return until dusk. I helped Sonam to prepare lunch for the villagers, and at midday I carried the heavy, warm dough and radish out to where the men were working. It took me almost an hour to reach the clearing in the woods. I followed the course of the silent river, walking far beyond the fork in the footpath which marked the beginning of the steep climb to Rizong. The days were now very still. I began to feel almost suffocated by the heavy grey clouds and the high valley walls. The silence seemed oppressive. I had the uncomfortable, slightly panicky feeling that it was closing in around me.

At first I was exhilarated by the cessation of noise. I felt tremendously free. My thoughts took on a sharpness, a clarity. Momentarily I was in control as I again experienced a sense of real integration. For months I had been pushed hither and thither by the mass of impressions and experiences which assailed me from every direction. But almost imperceptibly the space opened up by silence dissolved. Silence itself now assailed me from every direction. It seemed to creep up on me. I was afraid of pausing for breath on the footpath. I kept walking, deliberately crunching twigs underfoot and seeking reassurance in the creaking of the wicker basket strapped to my back. Occasionally I would startle a flock of shy birds which scurried beneath the trees, picking at the dusty earth. The birds were hard to see; they had no distinctive markings, but they blended closely into the parched, almost colourless landscape. The sound of my approach sent them skidding across the ground, and, with a great flurry of dry leaves, they disappeared into the woodland.

It was with some relief that I drew close to the place where the village men were working. Their shouts and laughter carried far across the thin, still air; and the column of smoke I saw hanging in the pale sky indicated their location among the trees. The villagers called out; but I knew their delight was more at the prospect of lunch and a break from work than at seeing me.

They were cutting wood within sight of Lababs, the collection of crumbling buildings where the eccentric *chomo* lived. The women had made themselves scarce; but this did not prevent the familiar fund of stories being reworked and passed back into circulation. I knew the men had me in mind when relating them. They were warning me about the fate of a *chomo*; for them it was a negation of the very freedom that I sought within that role.

Immediately the men began to gather around me, helping to unload the contents of my basket as the bursar shouted to the boys to stoke the fire and prepare fresh tea. Everyone settled around the fire, but there was something in the behaviour of the villagers which made me suspect a struggle was going on with the bursar. Certainly I could see that the men were determined not to be harried by him and, after they had finished eating, I watched them pull out from the pockets of their coats an assortment of half-made boots, coats and trousers.

I had forgotten that the Ladakhi New Year was only a few weeks away. It was important that the new outfits be finished since everyone was expected to dress up for the celebrations. Part of the villagers' resistance to the bursar on this occasion, I learned, was caused by his delay in giving them the pieces of cloth or leather which they had requested. Now the men were anxious about whether the garments would be completed in time; and a sort of silent war was being conducted between them and the bursar.

I was fascinated by the dexterity of the village men. Their value to the monastery was largely founded on their physical strength, but this masked many of their skills: I was surprised to discover how easily they moved from a morning of heaving and chopping firewood to such delicate sewing work. Everything they made was sewn from scraps which had to be carefully matched and pieced together. It demanded time and concentration. Many of the younger men were still learning, but they were impatient to finish the garments or boots they were sewing. Every so often, amid much laughter, one of them would hold up a hopelessly botched seam and plead for one of the elders to put it right.

The bursar knew that time was on his side. There was a limit to the amount of sewing work the men could do in the cold air. Their fingers became stiff and clumsy and, by slowly letting the fire burn low, he forced them to resume the work he wished them to complete for Rizong. He was not going to let me escape lightly either. I was put to work with the boys, sorting the smaller branches and dragging the bundles over to where the donkeys were being loaded.

I found it difficult to keep track of the time on days when the sun did not break through the thick cloud. I depended on the afternoon breeze to indicate the time for me to leave the woodland. Then I began the long climb to the monastery where the cattle were foraging for sparse vegetation on the high, rocky mountain slopes.

Eight

It was almost dark. The grey hue of the day was shading quickly into dusk, but a brilliant light illuminated the court-yard of Julichang. As I approached, shooing the cattle in front of me, I could hear loud, animated voices. The monks had returned from Yangthang.

Through the open door I glimpsed Memi Nasten and the other men from Rizong clustered close to a fiercely blazing fire. The dry twigs crackled and spat, sending flurries of glow-ing embers high into the night sky. The monks had brought us pieces of the food offerings which had been blessed during the ceremonies held at the village. They were stale, crumbling dough effigies, but this was not important – what mattered was the residue of ritual potency which they were believed to contain. The nuns carefully wrapped the pieces in cloth and tucked them into the front of their bodices. I did the same.

Memi Nasten watched me warm my hands over the fire. I could feel my cheeks begin to glow as the stinging cold gave way to a rapid infusion of warmth. Then, pausing in his con-versation, he turned to me and asked a single question: did the Indian authorities know I was living in the nunnery? It was the one moment I feared most of all. I had pushed the question of official permission to the back of my mind. The more I settled into the rhythm of nunnery life, indeed into the life of a *chomo*, the more it receded; but I had never succeeded in suppressing it completely. Now it was starkly posed. Instantly everything was transformed; what had seemed so secure only a minute ago, the experience of integration and harmony I discovered at Julichang, became fragile and chaotic.

It was impossible to answer Memi Nasten in the affirmative. I did not have a permit to be living in Julichang. I wasn't sure if Rizong and Julichang lay in a prohibited area and, although I had my suspicions, I had decided that it was better not to find out. Arriving at the nunnery had been very easy. It had not required any deception or subversion on my part.

From Leh I had caught a bus crowded with Ladakhi villagers, returning from a few days in the capital where they sold small amounts of surplus produce, mainly dried fruit and walnuts. The moment the vehicle pulled into the terminus, people had converged from all directions to push their way on to the bus. Several tried to clamber in through the windows or to push great baskets and bedding through them in order to reserve a seat; but I had stood back, watching nervously as my baggage, wedged among sacks of assorted goods and cans of kerosene, was strapped to the roof. Somehow I had squeezed myself into the mêlée of passengers travelling home. My journey was in the opposite direction. I was leaving behind a familiar world and I did not know my destination. The bus had jolted and rattled across the great dry plains, weaving its way through narrow valleys as we drove westwards from Leh. I did not come across roadblocks or checkpoints along the way and, after almost three hours, I got down at a tiny roadside settlement which I had been told marked the beginning of the footpath to Rizong. I followed the river valley, heading northwards between the mountains. What I remembered most was the violent heat and glare of the midday sun and, without the protection of cloud or shade, it had beaten remorselessly down upon me as I walked up the long dusty track to the nunnery.

My arrival at Julichang now seemed a world away.

Looking sternly at me, Memi Nasten warned that I was bound to be eventually located in Ladakh by the Indian police. They were reputed to be harsh on foreigners who broke the rules and he reminded me that if a warrant was issued for my arrest I would be in serious trouble. For the protection of Rizong's communities as much as for my own safety, he advised me to travel to Leh and inform the police of my whereabouts.

Deep down I knew this marked the end. It was a futile task

to try and persuade the Indian government to legitimate my presence in a sensitive area. That was why I had not tried earlier. I had been willing to take the risk of living there unofficially, not in hiding but maintaining a discreet profile. I no longer had this option.

I retreated to the kitchen. My immediate feelings were bitter. I felt betrayed; but the anger and disappointment sprang not from the fact that my "work" as an anthropologist had been placed in jeopardy, since I had long ago lost any interest in recording the kind of information which could be stored in notebooks and swapped in academic seminar rooms. It came from something else: a desire to protect an experience which was much less tangible, but infinitely more precious. I was edging slowly, at first cautiously, then with increasing certainty, towards an understanding of the disparate parts of my past. It was a vision of myself which initially surprised me by its clarity and power; but its source lay in the integrated life I had found at Julichang. Removed from my own society, from its constraints and complex relations, I was free to excavate aspects of my life, to clear away much of the debris, and to perceive more clearly its contours and direction. If I could somehow hold on to the sense I had begun to have of myself as an active, creative agent, I believed in the possibility of a future of my own making.

Sonam saw that I was stunned by what had just happened and she talked calmly, trying to reassure me that all was not lost. The police were bound to be sympathetic. After all, how could anyone living in a nunnery pose a threat to national security? I listened quietly. I wanted to be persuaded. The idea that I would have to leave the nunnery and the life I had created there seemed inconceivable.

Later I lay awake in a freezing night, my thoughts racing back and forth, oscillating between resignation and the determination to resist defeat. I considered the different courses of action open to me. One option was to go to Leh and pretend to have cleared the question of permission with the police; but I would not have been able to bring myself to lie or expose the community to any further risk. There seemed no way out other than to face it squarely. I knew that the experience of living at Julichang was so sharp and powerful that I could not let it go without exhausting every possibility. What I did not know was that this resolution would be incomprehensible to everyone I dealt with in authority. It could only be construed as highly suspicious.

I awoke to hear the nuns moving about outside. The day began as all previous days and the bursar arrived early. He was pragmatic, urging me to leave for Leh the next day and return quickly since he was depending on my help in the preparations for the New Year. I decided to delay my departure, however, until after the wedding.

There had been a good deal of whispered discussion among some of the monks and nuns about the marriage soon to take place between a young woman from Yangthang and a man from one of the neighbouring villages. Weddings were arranged. The two families involved spent many months reaching an agreement about the kind of dowry to be paid and finding an auspicious day for the ceremony to take place. I wasn't surprised to hear local affairs being discussed, but I was puzzled by the fact that every conversation about the marriage was shrouded in a mysterious, almost secretive, air. It seemed that the nuns were preparing to receive the bridal party at Juli-chang; and, once again, this meant protracted negotiations with the bursar about the kind and quantity of food to be served to the wedding guests.

I sensed that the wedding was important for the monastery, but could not be recognized as such. The monks had renounced ties which bound them to a human world of attachment, suffering and impermanence. The problem was that the spread of the Buddha's teaching depended on the continuity of the monastic order. The monastery had to sanction marriage unofficially. It gave gifts and food to the newly wed couple; but it was utterly forbidden for any of the monks to be present at a ceremony or wedding party. On an occasion of marriage the nuns acted as the intermediaries between monastic and lay life.

Once the bursar had supplied us with flour, rice, sugar and vegetables, we set to work preparing for the wedding guests. It was a relief, though, to be spared the monastery's close supervision of our work, since the bursar and all the other monks scrupulously avoided anything connected with the marriage celebrations. I tried to shut out the prospect of the journey to Leh. It was difficult. The ease with which I worked alongside the nuns, the bonds forged between us as a community, the feeling of my belonging there – all this was now heightened and served to exacerbate the fear that it was about to slip through my fingers.

The experience of integration I had found here derived from the harmony of the community in which I lived. This had intrigued me from my first weeks, since it was in sharp contrast with the atmosphere of bickering and rivalry which pervaded the Dharmsala nunnery and which had been so demoralizing. I genuinely failed to perceive tensions between the women at Julichang. Of course, Dondrup was sometimes cantankerous and she often grumbled; but it was accepted and never discussed as if it were a threat to the communal peace. I had expected gossip and irritation to break out periodically, given the confines of their lives and the constant demands made upon them by the monastery. But I began to understand that despite the many years of living and working in close proximity, each woman retained a separateness, an autonomy. There were no intimacies between the nuns. They addressed one another only by their formal, impersonal religious names. Most of all, it seemed to me, they took enormous care not to infringe on each other's space. Sonam's domain was clearly marked. It was the kitchen. Other nuns intruded occasionally and only with good reason, but they never lingered in the kitchen, quickly returning to their own particular corner of the courtyard or workroom. The identification of nuns with certain places was associated with the work in which they specialized; but this was not fixed. It changed every few years as the different posts within the nunnery rotated between the women.

The nuns were free from the clutter and claustrophobia of ordinary human relations. Their lives were dominated by unremitting physical labour for the monastery. But I now saw that this was what defined their spiritual persona. The women had both dignity and strength; and they were not unaware of it. Tibetan Buddhists might have in their cosmology a plethora of gods and deities whose powers could influence their lives, but the human condition itself remained filled with possibilities. For the nuns there was certainty in rebirth. The next stage in the journey towards nirvana was their rebirth as a monk.

Nine

A heavy, dark sky hung over the wedding day. It was one of the coldest days yet. I swept the dry leaves from the entrance to Julichang and carried out the low tables for the guests. We expected the groom's party at midday. Sonam told me that the men would not enter the nunnery, but they would be entertained outside, on the footpath which ran from the Leh road to Yangthang.

In common with all weddings, there was great anticipation. The morning seemed interminable. We waited and waited, straining to catch the first sounds of music which heralded the approach of the bridegroom and his entourage. There were several false alarms, when we ran excitedly to look over the wall of the courtyard, but saw only the empty dust track, stretching endlessly into the distance. Then, sure enough, we instantly forgot our impatience as the sweet tone of a flute disturbed the morning's silence and the muffled, steady beat of a drum reverberated through the long, narrow valley. We watched the slow progress of the party as it wound its way towards us. The musicians were at the head. Behind, flanked by a collection of kinsmen and villagers, were the groom and his attendants. From far away, it was the brightly coloured sashes tied tightly around the men's waists which first caught my eye. These secured the small silver boxes containing charms that each person carried to ward off evil spirits. As the party drew near, however, I saw that the groom and his supporters were magnificent, confident and proud in their heavy silk brocade and elegant hats. Apart from their special dress, the other men in the wedding party sported their best hats, dusted and placed squarely on their heads. I suspected that they would not stay that way for long.

I marvelled at Ladakhi hats. In defiance of the restrictions imposed on them by geography and climate, the local people were extravagant with their hats. Styles abounded. Some hats were tall, narrow and pointed; others were broad and squat. Their design seemed to contradict their purpose. Hats never fitted down securely around the ears to conserve heat, but they perched precariously on the crown of the head as the wearer went about routine work in the fields. Continual stooping and carrying, and the hazard of sharp gusts of wind, loosened headwear but miraculously never seemed to succeed in dislodging it entirely. No one went bareheaded. There were distinctive styles for men, women (married and single), children, monks and nuns. In fact, for monks there were up to twenty-two different kinds of hat, the choice being strictly governed by the occasion. I never discovered the reason for this abundance, but it was clear that Ladakhis were serious about their hats. The most striking was the headdress, studded with stones of turquoise and amber, of married women. It was passed between mother and daughter at marriage and was considered to be the major item of a bride's dowry; but despite its value, it was worn by women as they went about their everyday tasks in the fields and household.

Samsten and Sonam called out and waved from behind the high wall which ran along the footpath, but as the party approached they hurried down to the entrance to greet them. Tsodpah, struggling under the weight of a heavy urn, placed the beer outside, in the middle of the track, and I followed with bowls of barley flour. We were ready to begin.

An elaborate dance by the groom and his men opened the proceedings. The musicians started up a lively tune and the dancers slowly circled the pot of beer, dipping their finger-tips into it and casting drops widely into the air. They were making offerings to the gods and spirits. For Buddhists, a wedding was full of contradiction. Everyone knew it, but tried to make the best of the occasion by generating positive merit.

The nuns looked on as the beer flowed, loosening tongues and warming the chilled bodies of the villagers. The atmosphere relaxed into friendly banter between the women and their guests. Dondrup was anxious not to miss the chance of a few bowls of beer, particularly since she could spend the rest of the afternoon sleeping it off; but I declined to drink, because I needed a clear head and a sure foothold in order to negotiate the perilous screes behind the monastery where the cattle now grazed. As the men became jovial, I watched the change in their appearance – their faces became red and glowing as the inner heat generated by the alcohol came up against the bitter cold of the winter's day. In contrast, the groom, his early confidence faltering, began to look apprehensive. Soon he would arrive at the bridge's village. It was foreign, almost unknown territory and he looked anxiously to his attendants for support. Not until he had successfully persuaded the woman's family to part with their daughter and had left Yangthang with his bride, was he safe. The groom was depending on the good humour of his party to smooth the way. Using handfuls of barley flour, the men mopped up the last dregs of beer from their bowls and, stuffing the balls of alcohol-soaked dough into the front pouches of their coats, they set off, somewhat unsteadily, for the bride's village. The noise of their chatter died away as the grey afternoon closed around them. The nunnery was desolate once more.

We cleared away the tables and went indoors. Again we had to make preparations – to bake bread, to chop and season vegetables, to sift quantities of rice – for the next day the groom would return with his bride to feast on food provided by the monastery, and cooked and served by us. We had just settled into a routine of work when we were interrupted by the arrival of the monks from Rizong. They were on their way to Saspol, the village of Tsultim Nyima, the monastery's founder, which was some ten miles away. The monks were going to perform household ceremonies and they carried with them great bundles of butter, salt, and flour. We supplemented their supplies by offering them part of the bread we had just baked. The accuracy of their timing almost caught us off guard. The speed with which they arrived after the departure of the wedding guests made me think that the monks had hidden at the fork in the footpath, waiting there until they heard the noisy party pass on its way to Yangthang; but I could not know for sure. Memi Nasten arrived late. He appeared in the doorway of the kitchen and everyone moved to make space for him. I hadn't seen him since the conversation about permission; but he had refused the request I had made through Rigdol to write a letter to the police on my behalf. I bitterly resented him.

The heat and commotion in the kitchen were oppressive to me and I longed to escape to the mountain path. For the time being this was impossible. I would only draw attention to myself if I got up and left the room, using the excuse of the cattle. I had no choice, but to continue working by the stove, wishing I was invisible or, at least, hoping to go unnoticed. To my relief, Memi Nasten ignored me. The monks did not stay long. They were anxious to reach the Leh road before dusk. Soon afterwards I left for Rizong.

I walked steadily, hoping the exertion of the steep climb would dispel my anger. Confused thoughts were spinning in my head, sapping my strength; and yet I needed to conserve it at all costs. I had to convince myself that everything was not lost. That day, though, there seemed to be a conspiracy against me. For the first time the cattle refused to co-operate. The cows were infuriating, scattering over the mountainsides and frustrating all my attempts to drive them down to the nunnery. In near darkness I had finally reached the fork in the path when suddenly half the herd darted into the woods and disappeared from sight. I heard the crackling of brittle twigs under their hooves, but I could see nothing beyond the edge of the trees. I quickly rounded up the remaining cows before they could follow, and I hurried back to Julichang to rouse Dondrup.

During the afternoon she had drifted into a benign alcoholic haze. Now, cursing me violently at such a rude awakening, she set out with Tsodpah and Tsultim to search the woods for the missing cattle. They feared that the animals had wandered towards the river, straying in the darkness on to the ice and finding themselves stranded overnight; moreover, the weight of the cattle could easily break the ice and they would be plunged into the freezing water. This was an ordeal they rarely survived.

Much later that evening, the nuns and Dondrup returned. The cattle were safe. But the episode had been unsettling. It made me aware of how easily my presence could disrupt the equilibrium of nunnery life; and the unresolved question of permission lurked in my mind, casting a dark shadow over everything.

The valley remained sunless and closed. Not even the return of the marriage party, having successfully captured the bride, could relieve the foreboding chill of winter. It permeated our lives. The straggling party arrived at Julichang. At the head were the braver ones, the musicians, the groom, and his attendants; behind followed kinsmen and relatives. Last of all came the bride. We had been waiting eagerly to see her. The high spirits of the previous day had dissipated and the villagers were tired and subdued. After a night of merrymaking their mood had turned to one of quiet sobriety. The bride's copious weeping served to remind us of the uneasiness of the day.

The men looked rather wearily at the pot of beer brought by Tsodpah, but the piercing cold and the long trek from Yangthang had sharpened their appetites. With great gusto they began to tuck into the plates of food, but the bride ate nothing. Her sobbing continued. She sat apart from the group, her face covered and shielded from our gaze by one of her relatives. But I found my attention being drawn back to her, shocked at the violation, the trauma of her ordeal. Although the nuns could not know the pains of lay life, they approached her with great gentleness. I watched as Samsten bent over her shivering, huddled body and, speaking in a low voice full of kindness, she tried to persuade the bride to warm herself by drinking a bowl of tea. Sonam, who stood beside me, seemed uneasy while Tsultim, her face set and pale, gazed impassively ahead almost as if she had shut out the scene before her. The men were hungry and quickly devoured what had been put in front of them. As the party prepared to take its leave, the men crowded around the nuns and pressed money into their hands. One or two hurried to get the donkeys ready, checking the heavy loads which were strapped to their backs. From Yangthang, they had carried items of household furniture and kitchen utensils. These were the bride's dowry, the foundations of her married life.

The bride hung back until the men and the donkeys were a distance along the dust track. She embraced each nun, silently clinging to them, before she followed her husband to begin a new life in his village. An hour later I walked down that same dust track to catch the bus to Leh.

Ten

It was dark when I reached the capital. My Tibetan friends were surprised to see me and a little worried, fearing I might have fallen ill or that winter had defeated me. Neither of these would have been unexpected. Although they had been

impressed by the ease with which I had adapted to life at Julichang, they could not understand how I could speak with such
enthusiasm about it. Sonam and the other women were
regarded with a mixture of affection and amusement. The
harshness of the nuns' lives, and the physical stamina it
demanded, earned their respect. All the same my friends could
not help feeling that Ladakhi nuns were backward, illiterate
and uneducated. Explaining to them the reason for my unexpected trip to Leh, I did not dwell on the question of a permit
or express any of the fears I had about acquiring one; but the
next morning I was full of apprehension as I set out for the
police headquarters.

Leh was bathed in brilliant sunshine and the extraordinary
light had a curious effect on my perception of space. I felt I was
standing in the midst of a vast plain: the wide, open flat land
seemed to have extended, to have pushed back the ring of
mountains into the far distance. Looking across to them, I
thought of my life at Julichang, hidden there, lying in a dark,
narrow valley filled with secrets.

I was told that the superintendent of police was away, undertaking an inspection of checkpoints in the countryside and his
return was not expected for several days. His deputy, however, agreed to see me. Unlike his boss, he was a local man
and I thought this might work to my advantage. As a rule,
Indian government servants dreaded a posting to Leh. It was
a place considered to lie beyond the limits of reasonable human
habitation; a harsh, cold, isolated region and one which would
have been long forgotten had it not held such strategic importance. The local people, with their butter-smeared faces and
relaxed, if pragmatic view of personal hygiene, horrified visitors from the plains, particularly upper-caste Hindus. The
superintendent, I learned, was a Brahmin from Uttar Pradesh.
He was bound to be impatient and disgruntled.

The deputy superintendent told me that he was not sure of
the rules. He listened carefully as I put my case to him, but he
could not help smiling at the strange request. It was difficult
for him to envisage anything worse than living with Ladakhi
nuns and he kept repeating the word "*chomo*", obviously relishing the picture of an educated young Englishwoman living
among what he regarded as a collection of flea-ridden, frustrated old maids. He could not have imagined, though, what

it meant to me and the intensity of my desire to return to Julichang. I was no longer tormented, tossed hither and thither by
conflicting feelings. I was now determined to get my way; and
in this mood I interpreted the deputy's reluctance to commit
himself as tacit acquiescence.

There was just one more step, the approval of the district
commissioner which I believed to be a formality. The permit
seemed almost to be within my grasp. I had not dared to hope
that it would be so easily acquired.

The commissioner was a slow, ponderous Indian bureau-
crat. He questioned me in a rather bored, prefunctory way
until a telephone call interrupted the conversation. It was the
superintendent of police. He had returned unexpectedly to Leh
and on hearing of my request, he was anxious to assert his
authority. Julichang lay within a prohibited area and, as a
foreigner, it was out of bounds to me. There was no question
of a permit being issued. The commissioner shrugged his
shoulders; the question had been conveniently decided for
him. He dismissed me quickly, telling me if I wanted to argue
about it I would have to talk to the superintendent himself. Of
course, this was what I planned to do. The issue was not clear-
cut. It seemed that the rules of the Indian government defined
all areas lying a mile north of the Srinagar-Leh road as prohibited zones. In my estimation Julichang was borderline; it
lay about a mile from the road.

As I left the commissioner's office, one of his assistants
beckoned me to one side. To argue with the superintendent,
he told me, was futile. He had another plan. This involved
"negotiations" with the deputy superintendent, who had
initially been sympathetic and, given his knowledge of
Ladakh, might be more willing to interpret the rules as he
thought fit, rather than to be tightly bound by them. The
assistant promised to persuade him. In the meantime he suggested that I should quietly slip out of Leh and travel back to
the nunnery. I knew it was illegal. I had been forbidden to enter
the prohibited zone, but I decided, without much hesitation,
to follow this advice. The indecisiveness had stopped. I was
determined to return to Julichang, no matter what subterfuge
was involved. After all, what had I to lose?

I returned to the nunnery, half expecting to be stopped by
the police on the road out of Leh. The journey back echoed

my arrival many months before; but now it was impossible to recapture that mixture of excitement and adventure, the innocence of a beginning, which then so exhilarated me. The innocence was lost and the freedom of the beginning had changed into a certainty of the end. But I felt compelled to resist what, in my heart, I knew to be inevitable. I was knowingly breaking the rules and it made me very uneasy.

I met the bursar on the footpath and he asked me about the permit. I replied that the matter was undecided and that I would have to travel back to Leh in a month for further discussions. I gave him no more details, but he seemed satisfied with what he heard. What mattered to him was that I was now available for work; New Year was barely two weeks away and the Festival of Lanterns, marking the birth of Tsongkhapa, the great reformer of Tibetan Buddhism, was shortly to be celebrated at the monastery. The bursar told me that he was on his way to see his sister, the ragged *chomo* who lived by the Leh road. Like me, she supplied a valuable pair of hands.

Dusk was drawing in. The nunnery was silent and deserted. Nervously I approached the tiny room off the courtyard which was the focus of our winter work. I could hear voices and laughter inside. I lifted the latch. The familiar acrid smoke hit me violently in the face and I was forced to step back. My eyes burned and filled with tears, but through a bleary gaze I could see everyone crouched around a pile of smouldering logs. There was great activity. Fleeces lay in heaps about the floor; some of the nuns were busy cleaning and combing the raw wool, others were spinning it into fine thread. The women greeted me warmly, squeezing closer together to make a space for me next to the fire. Dondrup pulled me down beside her and we all laughed. No one spoke about my journey. It was as if I had never been away.

Part Three
New Year

Eleven

The monks had returned to Rizong. Having concluded the household ceremonies at Saspol, they were getting ready for a long period of religious activity in the temple. It would be exhausting. Their minds and bodies needed to be prepared for the concentration demanded at this critical time. There was much more at stake than just the transition from one year to the next. At New Year, the monks had to reconcile the principles of orthodox Tibetan Buddhism with unorthodox Ladakhi custom.

Buddhism was not indigenous to Ladakh. It had first penetrated the kingdom in the centuries after Gautama's death; but, at that time, its hold over the local people was superficial and short-lived. Between this early period and the later establishment of a distinctive Tibetan form of Buddhism throughout the Himalayas, the faith itself underwent important transformations. Monasticism became the core of the Buddhist tradition and the teachings of the Buddha, delivered orally to his disciples, were consolidated by successive councils of monks into a body of texts, canons, and commentaries. In the drive to establish a scriptural tradition, though, different schools began to emerge as a consequence of debate and dissension between scholars over doctrinal interpretation.

One of the most important divisions to emerge was that between the Mahayana (or Greater Vehicle, the way to salvation for the many) and the Hinayana (or Lesser Vehicle, the way to salvation for the few). The divergence between these schools was also expressed in geographical terms. The areas of Southeast Asia – Ceylon, Thailand, and Burma – adhered to the older, more orthodox Hinayana tradition; while the Mahayana tradition encompassed areas of Central Asia – Tibet, Nepal, and Ladakh.

The Mahayana school combined metaphysical speculation with a system of elaborate ritual practice. Of greatest importance was the equal weight accorded to the qualities of wisdom and compassion. Buddhist wisdom was accumulated not for individual enlightenment, but for the practice of compassion, for the benefit of all beings. From this developed the concept of *bodhisattva*, the object of the Buddhist life – an enlightened being who continued to take rebirth in the world in order to teach others the way to salvation. Gautama was no longer understood as an historical figure, but became a cosmic manifestation – transcendental, eternal, absolute.

Mahayana Buddhism passed into the remote, mountainous terrain of Tibet in the seventh century and, from early on, it enjoyed royal patronage. Monastic foundations received protection and encouragement, they benefited from tax dispensations, grants of land and the nomination, by the crown, of villages responsible for their economic support. The spiritual power of the monks went hand in hand with the expansion of their economic and political influence until, finally, the challenge they posed to the old Tibetan order provoked a violent suppression of Buddhism in the ninth century. Those scholars who escaped to neighbouring Ladakh carried the doctrines and practices of the Mahayana school with them. Here they found conditions favourable for the establishment of the faith; and sponsorship by sections of the Ladakhi royal household ensured that, through the material support of the laity, the monasteries became once again centres for learning and spiritual practice. This meant that Buddhism was introduced to Ladakh from above. Slowly the faith percolated downwards, through the different layers of the Ladakhi population and eventually became incorporated into the lives of the ordinary villagers. The support of the latter, however, was crucial in the consolidation of monastic power. It could be achieved only if the monks were prepared to come to terms with aspects of the indigenous culture. The solution to these obvious contradictions required ingenuity. New Year, in particular, threw the inconsistencies into sharp relief. At times I was startled by what I saw.

The Ladakhi New Year fell in the tenth month (usually December) of the religious calendar around which the Tibetan year was organized. Although the local people lived, on the

left to right, Lababs Chomo, Sonam, Tsultim, Tsodpah
kneeling, Chimme

Damchos

Urgen

Lababs Chomo

Chuski

Dondrup

Tsering

Rizong monastery

Sonam

whole, according to this Tibetan or "new" calendar, they continued to mark the passing of the year according to the "old" reckoning, or what was sometimes called the farmer's new year. They were not particularly interested in the Tibetan New Year which came two months later (February or March), as it was primarily a monastic occasion. But the representatives of Tibetan Buddhist orthodoxy, the monks, could not afford to ignore the Ladakhi New Year. At this time two traditions collided and the monastery had to fight to retain supremacy. For the Gelugpa sect to which Rizong belonged, the problem was sharply posed. Its founder in the fourteenth century, Tsongkhapa, sought to recover certain features of orthodox Buddhism which had lapsed in the religion's accommodation with the indigenous beliefs and practices of Tibet. Although his reforms were based upon a return to the doctrine, the importance of the scriptures and an emphasis upon the monastic discipline, they did not exclude many of the less orthodox practices. But the coexistence of these two facets continued to be uneasy and this was recognized at New Year, when the victory of monastic Buddhism was re-enacted as an integral part of the rituals of transition.

The beginning of the struggle for dominance was symbolized by the Festival of Lanterns. It marked the death of Tsongkhapa and, coming on the twenty-fifth day of the tenth month according to the "new" calendar, it lay very close to the end of the "old" year recognized in Ladakh. The climax of the ceremony was at dusk, when I was told that a thousand lamps would be lit around Rizong. It was now only a few days away.

Its approach, however, was marred by the fact that one of the senior monks had fallen ill; and the nuns learned, from the novices who arrived one morning without the bursar to collect fresh milk, that the doctor had been summoned from Yangthang. There was anxiety about sickness occurring at this critical time and it gave focus to the mood of uncertainty which I sensed as the New Year drew near. After lunch Sonam asked me to take butter and newly baked bread to Rizong. Had I not known otherwise, I would have assumed that the monks were away. No one called out to me as I climbed the last part of the winding track which led to the maze of cells. Here I usually met monks and exchanged greetings with them on the crooked stone steps as they carried fresh tea back to their rooms from the kitchen. They fasted after midday, but the rich butter tea sustained them in the long cold hours of study and meditation. Each monk had his own cell. It was built on two levels. The upper part was a balcony facing south and open to the elements. During the day the monks sat here, reading their religious scriptures in the sunlight. But now they had gone into retreat, retiring into the dark, enclosed lower levels of their cells to avoid distraction. From deep within the monastery came the familiar low, continuous murmur – the prelude to meditation.

Tiptoeing, I threaded my way through the narrow passages to reach the bursar's verandah. I found him in conversation with the doctor. Both men were speaking in hushed tones, taking care not to disturb the atmosphere of concentration. The doctor was sifting through his herbs and medicines, identifying various substances for the bursar. A strange-looking collection of roots, leaves, barks, rocks, dried flowers, and glass bottles of coloured liquid lay on the ground around him. To an untrained eye, it was a confusing mass of ingredients, but the doctor was an expert. He knew each item, its qualities, the possibilities of combination and transformation. His skill lay in synthesis, in his ability to forge a creative substance from the different elements he selected for the cure.

I approached cautiously. I had seen the doctor with his bags of medicines and collection of texts several times before at Rizong. We had never exchanged anything more than a few words. He held himself aloof – not only from me, I noticed, but also from the village men. The Yangthangers, in turn, expressed ambivalence in their attitude towards him. The doctor's special knowledge set him apart from the ordinary people and he was too closely identified with the monastery for them to feel comfortable in his company.

The bursar was not his usual buoyant self; I found him to be rather subdued, even anxious. The illness hung over Rizong. It would need all the power the monks could generate to push back its advance. Last year I had seen how quickly death came. The crucial moment, when victory seemed possible or defeat inevitable, approached much earlier than I had expected and in Dharmsala I had, with everyone else, watched helplessly as one of the nuns slipped towards death. Death meant disintegration, the final separation of elements and the enormous problem of rebirth. Although the nun's corpse had been quickly disposed of through cremation, there was a dangerous intermediate stage, a period of forty-nine days, in which the monks had sought through concentrated ritual practice to supervise the difficult transition between dying and rebirth.

I surprised the doctor by the interest I showed in his materials. Tibetan medicine was not unfamiliar to me as some of its renowned practitioners had followed their spiritual leader in seeking refuge in Dharmsala after the 1959 Chinese invasion of Tibet. I had rented a room from one of them, Yeshe Dhonden, the Dalai Lama's personal physician; and, from time to time, I had tried some of his treatments myself. For almost a year I had been able to watch him work, seeing patients, making diagnoses of illness and preparing his own medicines.

Tibetan medicine, codified in a body of texts, is an integral part of the much broader Buddhist cosmology. Instruction and training are given in the monasteries; and although it is unusual, it is not impossible for a lay person to practice as a doctor. In general, lay women are excluded from the medical training given within the monastic tradition; but a number have succeeded in establishing a reputation for themselves as unorthodox healers or as oracles.

Before 1959, when Rizong had enjoyed close ties with monasteries over a wide area of Central Asia, it had been the custom to send monks to Lhasa for spiritual instruction. The doctor told me that more than thirty years before he had accompanied one of the young abbots to Tibet and had himself studied there, until the flight of the Dalai Lama forced his return to Ladakh. Although he later married, he continued to practise as a doctor; now he was a widower and shared his time between Rizong and the village of Yangthang. During different seasons of the year, he travelled through the mountains and river valleys of the Himalayas, collecting the ingredients he needed for his medicines. He stored them in cloth bundles. These and the heavy volumes of texts seemed to be permanently strapped to his back. I never saw the doctor without either and their combined weight gave him a habitual stoop. On some occasions he consulted the texts, but most of his knowledge was carried in his head, accumulated during many years of trial and error.

The doctor planned to stay at Rizong until the crisis eased and the sickness was receding. I knew that the old monk had succumbed to a fever and, being unable to eat for many days, he lay weak and vulnerable. Crouching down beside the doctor, I watched him prepare medicines. Around him lay his materials – the ingredients and texts, a small pair of brass scales, several wooden bowls, a stone pestle and mortar. He began selecting and weighing quantities of leaves, bark, and flowers. These, he explained to me, would be crushed into fine powder and combined, sometimes using heat, with the various unidentified liquids stored in the glass bottles. The process of making the medicines was lengthy. It required great skill, but also a keen sensitivity to the fine adjustments which were necessary once the course of treatment was under way. The doctor was confident in his diagnosis. The next few days, however, would prove him right or wrong.

Each afternoon I met only the doctor and the bursar at Rizong. Occasionally I glimpsed one of the monks moving silently from the kitchen to the sickroom with a pot of glowing embers. The monastery remained closed, its inhabitants withdrawn.

Twelve

There was no peace at the nunnery. The quiet routine of our winter days was disrupted by villagers on the move. I felt excitement growing at the prospect of the New Year celebrations. The villagers brought their high spirits with them into Julichang and we could not help but be affected by their restlessness. The less pious were making their way home to prepare for New Year; others, in the middle of their winter journey around Ladakh's monasteries, set up camp in the woods nearby. Groups of families often travelled together, arriving with their heavily laden horses at dusk. There was always a good deal of noise as the men in the party set to work unloading the tents and unpacking their cooking utensils. They dispatched the children to search for firewood and we would hear them calling to one another as they played hide-and-seek in unknown territory. Once a fire was burning and the camp established, the women approached Julichang to request supplies – fodder for their horses, and butter, barley flour, and tea for themselves. They were nervous and hung back shyly as Tsultim took her keys to open the storerooms, but she was, as always, generous and she filled their hands with foodstuffs. Sometimes I saw her take items from the pouch of her own coat to give to them.

The pilgrims came from different parts of Ladakh. The variations in their appearance and dress were fascinating to me. Many had travelled from the remote border areas where the upheavals of history were expressed in the striking physical and cultural heterogeneity of the people. Sometimes I forgot how strange I appeared to visitors until I noticed them watching me and nudging one another. The curiosity was mutual.

I relied on the nuns, usually accurate in their assessment of visitors, to relay the news brought from afar. The women were always anxious to establish where the pilgrims came from, to acquire details of their villages, crops, households; but they were also eager to hear stories of the winter pilgrimage and the blessings the pilgrims might have received from learned monks; the different monasteries and settlements visited; the other pilgrims they met in the course of their travels. Information seemed to be readily exchanged and it was the endless variety of travellers to Julichang which helped the nuns to acquire an impressive range of knowledge. This had been obvious to me from my first days at the nunnery and it was constantly underlined in my conversations with the women, particularly with Sonam. I had come to rely upon the soundness of her judgement and to respect her understanding of the world. It was indeed remarkable, for, unlike the monks who covered huge areas of Central Asia in the course of their trading and religious activities, the nuns rarely travelled. Perhaps once in their lifetime they had even made the pilgrimage to India. And yet I never discovered anything inflexible or narrow in their outlook despite the restrictions and geographical insularity of their lives.

The pilgrims spent their days in the woods, delaying their visit to Rizong until the Festival of Lanterns. From the summer kitchen where I slept, I heard voices rising from their camp late into the night and I was soothed by the gentle rustle of animals stirring on the dry ground.

On the morning of the festival, however, I was woken before dawn by the sound of activity outside as the pilgrims prepared to set off for Rizong. I expected that we would be hurrying to finish our chores so that we too could soon leave for the monastery. But there was no haste at Julichang and there seemed to be time for everything. I sat in the kitchen with Sonam as she worked at a leisurely pace. She told me that the nuns were planning to reach the monastery in time for the midday meal; but she did not add what I and everyone else knew, that if we arrived early we would be sent by the bursar to help out in the kitchen.

Our small party of five noticeably swelled the numbers visiting Rizong. In contrast to the celebration of Namgyal Stonchok only a month before, there were few people attending the Festival of Lanterns. The majority of villagers had stayed at home, preferring to supervise last-minute preparations for New Year. This time we were not shown into the temple as I had expected; but the bursar led us through tight passages and up steep twisting staircases into the very heart of the monastery. I followed the nuns. We climbed steadily, but I quickly lost my bearings and I was not at all sure where we were in the maze of rooms. Suddenly we came into the private quarters of Shas Rinpoche, one of Rizong's absentee abbots. We were in the upper reaches of the monastery, in rooms I had never known existed, so well were they hidden from the rest of Rizong.

There was a small temple, a private room for meditation and a chamber where visitors were received. Although the windows were partially shuttered, harsh light streamed in through them. They had glass panes, something I had seen nowhere else in the monastery. Everything was beautifully ordered. The walls were decorated with painted silks, an altar of fresh offerings was set out in each room and the suite's arrangement gave the impression that the Rinpoche's return was expected at any time. Only the distinct chill of the air betrayed its many years of emptiness.

The bursar led us through the reception chamber and, pushing against a heavy wooden door, he revealed an open balcony beyond. Here Memi Nasten and the monks sat beside a simple altar, waiting for food to be brought from the kitchen. I stepped on to the uneven stone flags, feeling almost giddy at such a height. The ground dropped sharply away below the balcony and we had an unrestricted view across to the jagged peaks in the far distance. For the first time we truly saw beyond that dark, immutable wall of rock which shut off our world. I sensed a moment of lightheadedness among the nuns as they too stepped out into the thin, mountain air.

We were invited to sit alongside the monks for lunch. It had never happened before. In the temple, we usually hid in the shadowy recesses and crouched awkwardly on the floor behind the rows of monks. The temple was intimidating and I always felt the nuns were forced almost to cower before the tremendous authority of learning and concentrated ritual practice it contained. But it was different on this high, open balcony. We were not intruders into an enclosed, magical arena cluttered with objects whose potency only the monks knew how to release.

The doctor also joined us for lunch. He was still resident at Rizong, but the ailing monk was showing signs of improvement under his care and he expected the patient to be strong enough to take up his place, for short periods, in the temple at New Year. The monks heard the news with relief. The consternation provoked by the illness at last began to die down and they could now turn their attention fully to the problem of the New Year.

I stayed behind on the balcony with the nuns after the monks had retired to their cells to study and meditate and to prepare themselves for the ceremony which began at the end of the day. We helped the boys to clear away the debris from the meal, sweeping the stone floor thoroughly and watching meanwhile for the appearance of crows overhead. They were the scavengers of death and would be tempted to swoop on the balcony if stray crumbs were left scattered. We did not dare take such a risk. It would bring the wrath of the monks down on our heads and return the community to the uneasiness so recently associated with sickness and the threat of death.

I struggled to balance the pile of plates I carried, hurrying to keep up with the boys as they showed us the way back to familiar territory. We found the bursar waiting for us in the kitchen. He was agitated. He did not believe in leaving the New Year preparations until the last minute and it was his good fortune to have us captive at the monastery until the lamps were lit at dusk. The nuns, well used to the bursar's routine, busied themselves with the work and politely ignored him. It was not so easy for me to do this and I was often in the awkward position of being singled out as the audience for his complaints. I was sure that my willingness to play this role, to listen, was the explanation for the bursar's uncharacteristic outbursts of generosity. The bursar was anxious about the number of visitors set to besiege Rizong at New Year, the problem of feeding them all, of resisting their demands on his stocks. He told me that a particular day was set aside for each of the different villages associated with the monastery. The first day was for the nuns and Yangthang, the second for Hemis Shugba and the third for Saspol, though the latter were not expected to send a party this year.

It was difficult for me to know whether the bursar deliberately created the atmosphere of near panic in order to spur us on, or whether he was genuinely harassed by the responsibilities of his post. On this occasion, however, I was fortunate. Rigdol came to my rescue, and saved me from an afternoon of vegetable peeling by asking me to help prepare the ceremonial lamps which later would be used to illuminate Rizong. I sat outside the temple with three monks as we cleaned, polished and made new wicks for a thousand lamps. We worked with the constant hum of the recitation in our ears and I reflected on the fact that I had never done this kind of work for the monastery before. This and the gesture of admission the monks had made towards the nuns at lunchtime caught me by surprise, so accustomed had I become to our place as domestic servants. And yet I now sensed that we were being prepared for a different kind of role. Later, I came to understand it as an integral part of the monastery's struggle to retain control over its laity.

As the afternoon quietly slipped away, the nuns came to the temple to help us finish the work. By dusk one thousand lamps stood in rows on the ground and Rigdol supervised their filling with oil. I watched, thinking of Chuski, as the delicate aroma of the apricot kernel oil reminded me of our autumn days at Julichang. But the chilly mountain breeze quickly returned me to the winter landscape and in the gathering darkness I saw that the monks had congregated at the entrance to the temple. A hush settled over everyone as Memi Nasten lit the first lamp; and from its tiny, fragile flame the monks began to light all the others. They placed them on the ledges and sills at every level of the monastery.

The nuns prepared to return to Julichang. We were given lamps to leave at the sacred places we passed on our way down the mountain footpath. As we descended, we kept stopping to look back at Rizong. We imagined we would see it illuminated. The monastery remained in darkness. The lamps vainly flickered against the sharp wind and their light was swallowed up by the vast night sky.

Thirteen

The days became hectic. We put aside the winter work and devoted ourselves entirely to preparations for New Year. The nuns took turns to spend the greater part of the day at Rizong, but Sonam usually persuaded me to stay at Julichang until midmorning in order to help her churn extra supplies of butter. Arriving later at Rizong, I would find the nuns hard at work in the kitchen, baking bread and preparing dough for the fried biscuits made specially at New Year. By lunchtime they were coated with a mixture of flour and soot from the fire, and their eyes were red and swollen. I never adjusted to the thick, pungent smoke which hung permanently over the kitchen. Its sharp edge always caught the back of my throat and, in no time at all, I was forced to flee, coughing and choking, into the air. The nuns managed as best they could; but the fatigue clearly showed in their faces.

I considered myself fortunate to be able to work on the terrace outside the bursar's suite. Sometimes I escaped from the monotony of my work by surrendering to the movement of clouds across the faraway mountain peaks; at other times I allowed myself to be distracted by my companion, Urgen. He was dressed in the same threadbare clothes that he had worn at the nunnery throughout the summer; his hat, battered and grimy, was perched at the familiar angle on his head. I watched it slowly slip down over one ear as the day wore on. Urgen was partial to beer and for this reason the bursar arranged for him to be carried from his room to the verandah so that he could keep him under supervision. I remembered how, when he lived at the nunnery, Urgen had kept the nuns amused by his sly humour and obscure puns. He laughed a great deal at his own jokes; but I was never sure then that I had understood them. This time, for once, I had no doubt. Urgen and I shared the same fate. He shrugged his shoulders and chuckled when he saw the dismay register on my face at the prospect of hours of grubby, tedious work. He grimaced and wagged a rebuking finger in the direction of the storerooms. The bursar held no fear for him. Already I had noticed that Urgen's sharp tongue made the bursar awkward and self-conscious, perhaps even aware of the absurd light in which he often appeared.

Urgen was a skilled tailor and during his stay at Rizong he sewed new robes for the monks, stitching together pieces cut from the thin strips of cloth we had dyed at the nunnery in the autumn. For New Year the bursar had asked him to make prayer flags. A combination of the relentless summer sun and the harsh, biting winter winds had reduced last year's flags to faded tatters. They hung like rags from the different buildings, their printed prayers long since lost to the elements.

Urgen waited patiently for his materials. Eventually the bursar emerged from his rooms, trailing yards of cheap, brightly coloured cotton he had bought in Leh. He was anxious to secure our approval of his choice. Newly purchased the material looked coarse, the colours garish; but the climate would quickly temper this gaudiness. I nodded my assent. Urgen grunted.

The bursar proceeded to give him very detailed instructions on the size of the pieces to be cut, the way the edges had to be sewn and the number of squares to be fixed to the line which suspended the flags between different buildings of the monastery. The printing of the flags was done by the bursar himself. Once Urgen had cut and sewn several pieces, the bursar brought his printing materials on to the verandah. From behind my pile of turnips, I watched these activities with interest. On another occasion the bursar had told me that in the past the monks at Rizong used to make their own paper and, with handcut wooden blocks, printed their own texts. Now the monastery's new texts were commercially produced and bought in Leh. The print may have been finer and more even, but the pages lacked the solidity and durability of the handmade type. I had seen most of the old printing blocks, discarded and half-buried beneath the sacks of grain and piles of fleeces in the bursar's storerooms. For the prayer flags, though, the bursar had retrieved one of them and prepared it for printing. It contained a series of magical words credited with great power; but the efficacy of these mantras lay in their utterance and in repetition, rather than in their meaning.

The bursar let me rest from vegetable peeling to help him print the flags. First of all he poured thick, black ink on to the wooden block. I pulled one of the squares tightly over it as he ran a heavy roller several times across the material and, taking care not to smudge the wet ink, we laid the strips of printed cloth along the ground to dry. Later the bursar asked some of the younger monks to string the flags up from the high roofs of the monastery.

Rizong's kitchen was situated directly beneath where we worked and in the corner of the verandah was an outlet for the wood stove. Throughout the afternoon the pleasant odour of freshly baked bread wafted up through this opening in the floor. The shaft gave the bursar an opportunity to eavesdrop on the kitchen conversation and from time to time he crouched down over the hole to see what was going on or to shout orders at those below. This amused Urgen and me. Every so often as he peered into the kitchen, a blast of smoke caught him full in the face and he was forced to withdraw hastily.

By dusk the nuns had completed their work. They helped me to collect the cattle and we all made our way back to Julichang. As we stumbled down the mountain path, the nuns began to anticipate the days ahead. Their excitement was palpable. It affected me too, but I clung to the impending celebrations. I dared not consider what lay beyond the New Year.

Fourteen

After the morning's routine tasks, the nuns assembled in the kitchen to watch Sonam and Tsultim mould dough effigies. With some coyness, it was explained to me that they were making models of the ibex, a Tibetan wild goat. Our goats had long, elaborate horns. Looking at them made the nuns giggle mischievously. Ten of these animals were set out between two butter lamps on a makeshift altar constructed over the stove. They would act as the guardians of the New Year.

There was much discussion between the nuns about what they had to do next. They were anxious to adhere closely to the established routine, since to deviate from it might upset the delicate harmony between different forces which came into play at the time of transition. The nuns took this responsibility seriously; but they carried out the prescribed rituals with ambivalence. The tension and uncertainty was expressed in the frequent eruptions of their laughter. They were conscious of the incongruity of the customs they observed. When I asked the nuns if similar rituals were conducted by the monks at Rizong, I provoked great hilarity in the kitchen. They replied that the monks had no need to concern themselves with such superstitions. But I knew this was only a partial answer to my question. It was obvious that the New Year practices at the nunnery were more than trivialities; and, although it was never made explicit to me, I could understand them at one level as the attempt to achieve intellectual order, to integrate the village practices or pre-Buddhist "leftovers" into a spiritual domain dominated by Buddhist monasticism. By delegating to the nuns the responsibility for carrying out these unorthodox practices, the monastery sought, through an accommodation of local custom and beliefs, to retain its hold over the laity, and at the same time preserve its own spiritual purity. I now saw clearly how the ambiguous status of the religious women made it possible for them to act as intermediaries between orthodox and unorthodox practice, between the monastery and the village; and yet it was as if their responsibilities at New Year sharpened the contradictions of this life, pushing the women almost to breaking point. The explosions came suddenly and violently.

Long after the festivities had been concluded, I puzzled over two things I never imagined I would see associated with monastic Buddhism – sacrifice and offerings to the dead. They broke fundamental tenets of the faith, non-violence and the Buddhist denial of a soul, a stable, enduring ego; and yet both were carried out in the nunnery at New Year. The more I reflected on what I witnessed, the more conscious I became of new, unknown facets in the lives of these religious women. At the time I was not sure what they meant or how they fitted into the image which had crystallized in my mind over several months; but the New Year had irrevocably changed my perception of the nuns and I knew that I could no longer be sure of my place in their world.

Rizong's flock of sheep and goats, about 150 in all, had been brought to the nunnery from grazing areas far afield. The animals were tended by Nordup, a young man from one of the neighbouring villages which paid labour tribute to the monastery. From the moment his flat feet had carried him into Julichang, Nordup was teased by the nuns. He puffed and wheezed, his great florid face glowing despite the grey chill of winter which had sapped the blood from our cheeks; but I soon discovered that his rich hue was caused by his consumption of beer, rather than by excessive physical exertion at the high altitude. Although Nordup was slow and lumbering, he was kindly. His real misfortune was to be in search of a wife. No one, it seemed, would have him and the nuns missed no opportunity to remind him of his failings as a suitor. I thought Nordup accepted the ribbing with remarkable patience and only occasionally did he try to snatch his revenge. He seemed to have resigned himself to living with the jokes until the spring when he returned to the summer pastures with Rizong's herd.

With the dough effigies installed in the kitchen, the nuns prepared to begin the next sequence of rites associated with the New Year. Bracing ourselves against the cold outside, we hurried to the sheds below the courtyard which housed the monastery's animals. In contrast to the sharp edge of yet another sunless winter day, the air inside the compound was soft and humid. The sheep and goats were bunched together, restless and impatient at their confinement. Nordup had gone ahead to separate those with white coats from the rest of the flock. These were the animals selected for sacrifice. Sonam and Tsultim pushed their way into the middle of the jostling flock and as Nordup strove to hold them down, the nuns daubed each animal with red dye and forced beer down its throat. There was a fierce struggle. The animals resisted and thrashed wildly, splattering everyone with both substances.

I looked on the scene nervously from the safety of the doorway. The nuns had not stepped over the threshold into violence; but, although it had been only a mock sacrifice, there was no doubt that their hands were bloody and unclean. We were all implicated.

It was impossible to leave for Rizong until we were cleansed; our impurity went beyond a surface smattering of dye and beer. It was deeply imbued. We returned to the kitchen to begin purification. Sonam handed out pieces of dough and, following the example of the others, I passed it over every part of my body. We threw the polluted scraps on to a pile of straw in the centre of the floor. Sonam sprinkled drops of beer over them and set the straw alight three times. As it smouldered, she scooped it up and carried it outside. To everyone's relief it quickly burst into flames and, as it destroyed the dangerous matter, our purity was restored.

We reached Rizong at midday and discovered that its atmosphere had changed, from the quiet withdrawal of the last days into noisy activity. The final stages of preparation were underway. The heavy doors of the temple were flung back and light flooded through the dark interior. Cool mountain air began to dissolve the thick, sweet aroma of incense which clung to the walls and ceiling. One of the younger monks was dusting the wooden cabinets of texts which lined the temple; a second was sweeping the aisles; a third collected offering bowls and burntout lamps; while a fourth was furiously beating the heavy rugs and cushions on which the monks sat during ceremonies. Occasional shafts of light caught the floating spirals of dust and, for a moment, we saw the temple through a kaleidoscope of colour.

But we could not linger. Other monks hurried past us along the narrow passages between their cells, the kitchen and the upper levels of Rizong. The bursar had seen us arrive and he called out from somewhere at the top of the monastery. As we followed his directions and climbed higher, wisps of smoke became visible in the pale sky. They rose from a woodfire which burned inside one of the small rooms tucked away above the temple. We reached the top of the stairs and, gasping for breath, we half-tumbled into the dingy room ahead. It was hot and smoky; but a delicious smell of cooked biscuits filled our nostrils. After a few moments, as my eyes adjusted to the light, I saw that almost all Rizong's monks were gathered in the room. The heat from the stove forced them back and they sat against the cool, clay walls. With speed and skill, the monks were rolling, twisting and moulding strips of dough for the New Year biscuits. Two of them stood close to the flames, tossing pieces of dough into a huge pan of hot oil, turning them over and over until they were lightly browned. Then they lifted the biscuits out, leaving them to drain and cool on a wooden rack by the door.

The heat emanating from the blazing logs stung the faces of the men working over the stove and I felt my own skin tingle, even though I sat at a safe distance. With such hot, volatile liquid they could not allow their concentration to waver for a moment. It was impossible to work for a long stretch in these conditions and the monks regularly exchanged places with one another. Those just released from frying the biscuits sought relief outside and, from my place by the door, I watched them as they filled their lungs with draughts of clear mountain air and mopped their ruddy, sweat-streaked face with the edge of their robes. They did not rest for long, but stepped eagerly back into the stuffy atmosphere of the workroom. The monks were relaxed and genial. I began to think that perhaps they, too, approached the New Year with some measure of excitement.

Almost as soon as we arrived, the nuns began to knead and plait the dough, their nimble fingers swiftly adjusting to the task. I was hopeless at anything demanding speed and agility; so, for once, I was content to be at the beck and call of the bursar, to run errands for the monks and to carry endless supplies of fresh tea from the monastery kitchen.

Later I took up my usual place on the bursar's verandah, sitting close to Urgen who was quietly mending the threadbare patches in the woollen blankets the monks would use during the temple rituals. The bursar, meanwhile, was busy in his storerooms, checking his stocks and ordering the boys to sort and stack certain items. They were barely able to lift the heavy sacks of grain and rice and we could hear the bursar's voice rising with irritation and frustration. Urgen warned me that worse could follow. He pointed out two tiny figures, emissaries from Yangthang, who were approaching Rizong from the mountain path. They had been sent on behalf of the village to collect luxury foodstuffs to be shared between the different households over New Year.

The bursar greeted the village men coldly. He did not let them enter his storerooms, but instructed the boys to bring various sacks out on to the verandah. His face was set in an unpleasant scowl as he silently handed over the items – salt, rice, sugar, cooking oil, and bricks of tea. The villagers refused to be intimidated by him. They stood firm, counting and then scrutinizing the contents of each bag before they strapped them on to the backs of their donkeys. Once they had collected a full load, the villagers did not hesitate, but set off at a brisk pace towards Yangthang. They gave the bursar no time to change his mind and call them back. The bursar looked over to where Urgen and I were working. There was still a sizeable quantity of turnips to be peeled. I steeled myself for an outburst of his anger; but Urgen was bold. He chuckled loudly and made sardonic remarks under his breath. The bursar snarled, but with some difficulty managed to restrain himself. He refused to be provoked and, retreating to the safety of his rooms, he did not reappear until he had collected himself. Urgen looked over to me and smiled with the smug satisfaction of a victor. We knew the bursar could not maintain his churlish demeanour in the face of everyone else's ebullience. Rizong was now bursting with excitement and anticipation.

One of the monks called me to the room where they had been making the New Year biscuits. The fierce flames, which earlier had crept up the sides of the stove, had subsided; but the glowing logs continued to radiate considerable heat. A mountain of sweet-smelling biscuits lay by the door. Some of the monks were dusting themselves down; others were modelling tiny animals out of the scraps of unused dough. When I looked more closely I saw that they were making effigies of the Tibetan wild goat. I was surprised. I thought these models were symbols of pre-Buddhist or folk beliefs; and yet these goats had turned up again, in the most unlikeliest of places, the monastery.

I was drawn into the speculations of the monks and nuns as to who would play the "goat man" in a particular village. Each year a different person dressed up as an ibex for the duration of the festivities. I was warned to be careful of the goat man; he was frightening and assumed strange powers. But I was not sure if the monks were having a joke at my expense.

Fifteen

It was the last day of the old year. From first light the nuns moved about quietly, whispering in low voices among themselves. There were no outbursts of laughter, no moments of lightheartedness. The early morning air was thick and heavy. Its raw edge gave a new brutality to the cold. Breathing was difficult, often painful. I had a sense of foreboding: but it seemed so closely intertwined with the harshness of the Himalayan winter that I could not be sure how real it was.

I sat around the fire with the other nuns. We ate our breakfast soup in silence. I looked anxiously at Sonam. She was subdued and preoccupied. We cleared away our bowls and I was sent back to the kitchen to watch over the fire. A small iron pot, its lid firmly wedged over the rim, stood on the stove.

Shivering uneasily I crouched close to the fire. The logs were smouldering but not fully alight. I tried blowing on the embers in an attempt to ignite the wood. Flames jumped erratically; but the damp logs refused to burn. Smoke was gradually filling the kitchen. I reached for Sonam's goatskin bellows and tried imitating the method I had seen her use every day to generate a draught. It was not as easy as it looked, but I persevered and eventually got the fire going. I was exhausted by the effort and covered with soot. As I rested against the stove, the contents of the pot began to cook and a familiar odour seeped into the room.

I could not resist lifting the lid to confirm my suspicions.

Inside I saw a rich, bubbling stew of meat and onions. I was puzzled. Both were forbidden to Buddhist devotees. Although I knew such prohibitions were disregarded in some of Ladakh's monasteries, Rizong was well known for its purity, its orthodoxy. Hitherto I had seen nothing which cast doubt on its reputation as a community adhering strictly to Buddhist principles. I felt uncomfortable. I stirred the stew occasionally and waited for Sonam to return. Eventually she appeared in the doorway of the kitchen, her face dour and pinched with cold. She said nothing, but picked up the pot from the stove and beckoned me to follow.

Outside I found the nuns huddled close together in the freezing air. Tsodpah was carrying a jug of beer, the others held bowls of bread, sugar, and curd. I was given three butter lamps. There was something about their pale, unsmiling faces which almost frightened me; but I said nothing and watched silently as Tsultim climbed the mountainside which rose steeply behind the nunnery. We scrambled over the loose rocks after her. She placed three flat stones on the dry earth and the offerings we carried were divided between them. Sonam ladelled a portion of meat and onions on to the surface of each stone and Tsodpah sprinkled drops of beer over them. I waited to see what would follow.

Suddenly, the women shattered the stillness of the winter day. They began to call out the names of former inhabitants of Julichang, nuns now deceased. Their voices were shrill and brittle, their chanting broken by wails and sobs. It was a violent outburst of emotion which echoed eerily down the long, dark valley.

I stood awkwardly, an onlooker at a scene which was frozen in the chill of the Himalayan air. It was one I could hardly grasp. I was familiar with the physical strain of the women's lives, their resilience and stoicism; but I had not anticipated this – an uninhibited expression of pain and grief. The precepts which bound their lives as religious devotees and distanced them from the uncertainties of household life had not made the nuns remote or austere. On the contrary, I recalled their gentleness with the Yangthang bride and remembered their sensitivity in other situations at the monastery and at Julichang.

But I was shaken by the weeping of the nuns. For a second

I perceived a frightening void, a chasm of bleakness and desolation. It was as if it had opened up before them and they hovered at its brink. Slowly their sobs subsided and the women regained their composure. They quickly covered the cracks which only a moment ago had laid bare their vulnerability. The outburst had left them defensive and self-conscious.

We sat on the cold, rocky ground and each of us pulled out a bowl from the front pouch of our woollen robes. Sonam gave us some of the meat and onions, followed by a small quantity of beer. No one spoke; but we cast nervous glances at one another as we consumed them. Tsultim divided the rest of the offerings. These, too, we ate; but a small amount of each was left on the three stones. The pots containing the remainder of the meat and beer stood nearby.

Chilled and pale, the nuns struggled to their feet. We were unsteady and our frozen limbs moved clumsily. We nearly laughed aloud but checked ourselves, fearful of upsetting the uneasy calm which had returned. Uttering a chorus of shouts and cries, the nuns implored the sleek black crows, hovering a distance away, to swoop down and devour everything we had left on the mountainside. We did not look back as we made our way in silence down the slope to Julichang.

The nuns appeared relieved. It was behind them for another year. They warmed themselves by the fire and prepared to meet the New Year. Their animation was restored and they were again the women whose life and work I shared. But I saw clearly on their blackened faces the traces left by their tears.

Sixteen

We were allowed to stay up late. For New Year's Eve the bursar sent candles and extra kerosene to light the nunnery after dark. The nuns gathered with their scriptures and rosary beads in the small room off the courtyard. They began to recite prayers they knew by heart. Their voices blended into a musical singsong, the unbroken rhythm almost hypnotic in its effect. Nordup brought a jug of beer and settled himself comfortably beside the fire. He tried to tempt me to join him. The appeal of the beer lay in its power to infuse warmth. I enjoyed the sensation of mild intoxication – the tingling cheeks, the burning in my stomach, the lightheartedness which could defy the weight of the winter chill. All day I had carried the chill of that morning on the mountainside. The stark picture of the weeping nuns filled my mind; and in an effort to dissolve its hold, I agreed to share the beer with Nordup.

Dondrup needed no persuasion and, propping herself up in a corner, she began to drink steadily from her bowl. She retreated from everything going on around her and refused to join in the nuns' prayers or in the friendly banter between Nordup and me. I had become used to seeing Dondrup, her tasks finished for the day, hunched over a jug of beer, a withdrawn and melancholy figure amid a room filled with work and noise. But on New Year's Eve I was more conscious of her as she sat in her grimy, patched coat and stared into the fire. Many times I had wondered what she was thinking when I saw her gaze held by the pattern of the flames and the rich glow of the embers. No one knew where Dondrup came from. Her past was unknown, except that one day she had arrived at the nunnery in flight from a violent husband. The nuns could not remember how many years had passed since then. They teased Dondrup when she was cantankerous and moody; but they were always careful not to violate her personal privacy. Often she fell asleep where she sat and we covered the solitary, threadbare figure with blankets to shield her from the extremes of the night air.

Dondrup was oblivious to the gaiety which filled the room. The combination of the beer, the hot, smoky atmosphere and the soporific effect of the nuns' chanting made it hard for me to stay awake. I could feel my eyes closing, but the occasional nudge from Nordup jolted me back into the noise and laughter of the room. I longed for my bed and the cool, still night air. There were only a few hours remaining before we set off for Rizong.

When we eventually retired, I slept fitfully. My head was full of thoughts and strange impressions. These had been provoked by the events of the last days; but the alcohol I had drunk tempered the sharpness of certain images. Different scenes became confused, juxtaposed or merged in my memory. In the half-light between sleep and wakefulness they seemed vivid, overbearing, invasive. I tried to resist sleep, frightened of being plunged into the turbulence of my subconscious mind.

I lay quietly, perhaps dozing, until I heard the nuns call from below. It was dark and bitterly cold. We had to reach the monastery before dawn. The rituals performed at Julichang had been only the preliminaries. Rizong was now poised to intervene. At New Year it displayed its power and wealth with dazzling splendour.

We waited by the entrance to Julichang, but Nordup did not appear. Tsodpah was sent to the room in which she brewed the beer. Here she discovered him and, with some vigorous shaking, managed to rouse him. Greatly amused, Tsodpah returned to tell us how Nordup, his hat still on his head, had been lying in the straw fast asleep, emitting loud, contented snores. Shortly afterwards, he shyly emerged. He was dishevelled and bleary-eyed, embarrassed at having to wash and smooth his crumpled coat under our scrutiny.

The nuns had exchanged their torn and stained working clothes for their finest red robes. For the first time they wore shoes and socks. Usually they went barefoot, even in winter, or they shuffled along in big, old boots. I noticed, too, that their skin had a pinkish tinge from scrubbing, as they had tried to remove some of the encrusted grime from their faces and arms. Even Dondrup had taken steps to smarten herself for the occasion.

On the instruction of Sonam I changed my overcoat. I wore the down jacket in which I had first appeared at the nunnery in the autumn. Sonam had taken one look at it then and told me to put it away until New Year. Despite its warmth, she advised me not to wear it every day because it would be quickly spoiled by soot and dust from the wood fire. Although this defeated the purpose of bringing the jacket, I accepted her advice. There had been, however, a single exception. At Sonam's behest I had worn the jacket for my audience with Memi Nasten, when I had sought his help in my approach to the Indian authorities. The jacket had brought me no luck and I had been glad to pack it away once more.

Most days I wore a Ladakhi coat which was like everyone else's, soiled and threadbare. I was ambivalent about the jacket and at New Year I felt rather uncomfortable in this near-pristine garment. But the nuns were very enthusiastic and they marvelled at the softness and lightness of its down filling. Dondrup kept prodding the jacket in disbelief; in her opinion, anything so light could not possibly keep me warm.

We set out along the mountain path. Nordup with his thick, heavy head lagged behind with Dondrup. Both struggled to keep up with the sprightly step of the nuns. I stumbled along, breathless and barely able to speak as I conserved every ounce of strength for the steep climb ahead. In the darkness it was almost impossible to see the way, but the nuns seemed to know every stone, every curve and incline on the path to Rizong. Their pace never slackened.

We came around the final bend in the footpath. Before us stood Rizong. Its outline was barely discernible against the night sky, but flickers of light from the temple broke through the darkness and caught the jutting edges of the monastery's whitewashed walls. The wide valley was resonant with the sound of the long trumpets summoning the monks to prayer. We could almost feel the vibration of the deep tones as they pierced the thin mountain air. The nuns quickened their step. We hurried to reach Rizong before the New Year ceremony began.

I followed the nuns into the kitchen. Here we rested and waited for Dondrup and Nordup to arrive. They staggered up the last punishing rise and, panting and wheezing, sank to the floor by the wood stove. Both were unable to speak. Nordup held his head in his hands and smiled weakly. He conceded defeat to the nuns; but their superiority was affectionate and mingled with humour. He knew he had only himself to blame for the excess of the previous evening.

The kitchen was empty. The bursar and the boys were absent; but baskets of vegetables and a row of gleaming pots stood at the side of the stove. They reminded us of onerous preparations ahead; this time, though, the nuns looked blankly at them and said nothing. Their attention was focused elsewhere. Afraid of dirtying or crumpling our clothes, we crouched in an uncomfortable position on the stone floor and waited to be called to the temple. The muffled sounds of footsteps hurrying above the kitchen ceased. The night was still once more. The nuns were tense, their bodies awkward and taut as they strained to catch every whisper which echoed in the silent valley.

We did not have to wait for long. One of the young boys was dispatched by Memi Nasten to bring us to the temple. He clattered down the steep stone steps into the kitchen. We immediately rose and hastily adjusted our dress.

I watched the nuns smooth their robes with evident pride. Their faces were flushed with excitement and I was conscious of their physical beauty. It was unveiled as the nuns, at last, were admitted to Rizong's temple as spiritual women.

We paused at the entrance. I caught my breath at the glittering spectacle which lay ahead. The dark, cluttered mysterious space had vanished. The interior was bursting with light. Kerosene oil, so carefully conserved by the bursar, fuelled the great glass lamps hanging throughout the temple. The dim glow of the butter lamps was swept aside by this fierce illumination, exposing every hidden corner and shadowy recess.

In the centre stood the statue of the Buddha. It was alone, uncovered and, for the first time, truly revealed. It was impossible to escape that silent, enigmatic gaze.

The nuns slipped off their shoes and crossed the threshold. Before us were rows of assembled monks. They were hushed and bowed beneath silk brocade robes. The weight and magnificence of their attire exaggerated their obeisance. I saw that the bursar was present, though I barely recognized him in his ceremonial dress. He has an air of spiritual dignity and solemnity I had never perceived in my dealings with him.

I tasted the sweet fragrance of the incense as I joined the nuns inside the temple. I looked around nervously, awed by the splendour of the occasion and the ostentatious display of Rizong's wealth and power. The doors of the temple were closed behind us. The night dissolved into memory and we entered another world.

The monks and nuns prostrated themselves before the great bronze figure, and began to repeat their adherence to the Buddha, the doctrine and the monastic community. Their voices hardly rose above a whisper, but the chanting had a momentum of its own, bridging the disjunction of time.

I lost my sense of duration in the temple. I was adrift, only conscious of the uncertainty of my perceptions. The light played tricks. Its penetration was refracted and scattered through the thickening haze of incense; its brilliance transformed into a deep hue as it reflected the rich golden silk worn by the monks. The soft murmur of faith enveloped me. It was dreamlike, elusive and strange.

The stinging cold air on my cheeks eventually roused me. It was filtering into the temple as the young boys drew back the heavy doors. The pale morning sky cast shadows through the interior. Dawn had broken and with it we had passed from the old year to the new.

Seventeen

Dazed and pallid, the nuns cautiously stepped outside. Dondrup, Nordup and I followed them on to the narrow balcony. The weak light of the early morning was soothing and we stood together with our backs to the great valley which fell away behind us. We drew in several deep breaths. The giddiness and disorientation with which we had emerged from the temple, slowly dissipated. The monks had remained inside to remove their ceremonial robes and, through the open doors, we heard the soft rustle of silk as the heavy cloaks were folded and packed into chests until the next occasion.

The bursar was the first to appear on the balcony. In his familiar attire and absorbed once more in worldly responsibilities, he seemed a lesser man. He was aware of the disparity and of our critical gaze. He shrugged his shoulders in a half-embarrassed gesture and ordered us to work.

We went down from the high balcony into the kitchen. It was draughty and dingy. The young boys were stoking the three wood stoves. The fires spluttered and smouldered and the boys tried vainly to stem the flow of smoke by energetically pumping the bellows in the base of the stove. Already their newly scrubbed cheeks were besmirched and their clothes soot-streaked as they struggled beneath the weight of heavy logs and large iron pots.

Food had to be cooked for almost fifty people. The bursar hovered anxiously over us. There was no time to be squeamish about the acrid smoke. We tried to ignore it, but it stopped up our throats and made our eyes well with tears. Once the fires began to burn properly, the air cleared and we had some relief; but then the kitchen quickly became hot and crowded. Those monks not occupied in preparing the temple for the next part of the New Year ceremony came to assist. Their presence, though, upset the hierarchy of command. The bursar was disconcerted and the efficiency of the nuns was thwarted by constantly changing orders. For an hour or so everyone fought to retain their patience and good humour as the work gathered pace.

Nordup helped me sift the rice while the nuns stood close to the stoves and watched over the pans as they cooked. Occasionally they stirred, occasionally they sampled their contents. Theirs was an unenviable task; sweat streamed down their faces and their foreheads were wrinkled and puckered by the concentration the work demanded. Gone was that proud, confident composure which had marked the nuns when they had arrived at Rizong before dawn. It was difficult to imagine that the temple ceremony had been only a few hours earlier. Daybreak had decisively broken its spell. The woman were now harassed and their once immaculate robes were smeared and awry.

Watching them at work, I found myself drawn back again to that scene on the mountainside when the nuns had made offerings to the dead. I wondered if the monks could have known of the extraordinary outburst such a ceremony had provoked. I didn't dare ask. The women themselves never spoke of that morning again; but the explosion was seared in my memory. It was a secret we all silently shared.

The Yangthang villagers were expected at midday. Entire families would make the journey to the monastery and stay overnight in the guest house. Everyone it seemed, except the bursar, looked forward to their arrival. I was excited. For the first time I would see the village women. Of course many of the men, their husbands and brothers, were well known to me because of their work at Rizong and at the nunnery during the late autumn. At that time I had watched the men use every spare moment the bursar gave them between tasks to sew and patch garments for their families to wear at New Year; and this activity had given some substance to the vague picture of the women I held in my mind. My other source of information was the nuns. They often referred to the hardships of the Yangthang women when contrasting lay responsibilities with their own lives as religious devotees. In particular, they talked about the burdens associated with the two primary roles of village women – marriage and motherhood. Without being very conscious of it, I had come to imagine the Yangthang women as overworked, stooped and prematurely aged.

It was difficult in the dark, shuttered kitchen to know how long we had been working; but gradually the monks dispersed and the pace slackened. With the contents of the pots simmering gently on the stoves, the nuns went outside to prepare themselves for the villagers' arrival. Squinting in the harsh daylight, they stretched their stiff limbs and brushed off the soot and dust which clung to their robes. We shielded our eyes against the glare and tried to catch the first sound of the Yangthang musicians or the first glimpse of the party as it wound its way up the steep path to Rizong. Most of the monks had gathered on the balcony outside the temple and they engaged us in a mock competition over who would sight the villagers first. We were hindered by Nordup who, having finally emerged from his early morning torpor, was irrepressible. He distracted us with his chatter so much that we neither heard nor saw the villagers as they turned the corner and came into view. A chorus of cries came from the monks, their shouts carrying down the valley and becoming blurred as the sounds mixed with the greetings called out by the Yangthang party. Far below us the villagers appeared as tiny dots on the landscape. They were closely bunched together and this made it impossible to distinguish between them; but, approaching the final ascent, certain members began to straggle and the group separated.

We were all looking for the goat man. Sonam nudged me and pointed to the middle of the party. There he was, hidden among the village men – a menacing figure with his long wooden stick, black mask, and thick fleecy coat. The nuns shrank back and tried to guess which villager it was. His disguise was so effective that they succeeded in identifying him only after a lengthy process of elimination. This year the goat man was played by the doctor's son.

The men, the musicians, and two decorated yaks heralded

the arrival of the party at the monastery. The women and children followed at a distance. They did not hurry to keep up with the others; but rested at each sharp turn in the path and caught their breath. Finally they came towards us. The exertion of the climb had filled their cheeks with colour and it enhanced their handsome, almost youthful, appearance. I was immediately struck by the confidence of the women and its reflection in their proud, yet graceful, bearing. Watching their arrival, their striking entrance and distinctive presence, I knew now why I had not seen the women before at Rizong. Their impact lay beyond the brilliant silks and heavy, ornate jewellery the women wore and I understood the danger these women posed to monastic celibacy. I noticed the keen interest among the nuns as they approached, their expressions mixing delight with admiration. The monks, however, were cautious and they moved away from the temple balcony which overlooked the verandah where the villagers had started to congregate. The sexes remained separate: the men stood together, close to the yaks; the women hung back with the children. Nordup left us and sought refuge among the men. We joined the women. I was anxious to look more closely at them; they, in turn, were keen to assess me.

The shrill tone of the musician's pipe and the beat of the drum faded away and the day became hushed and still. Memi Nasten appeared on the balcony above us. He began to recite blessings and to toss handfuls of rice, the symbol of fertility, over the villagers below. Two of the younger monks made their way down to the verandah with bowls of beer and butter. The yaks stood mute and docile as both substances were rubbed on their long, curly horns and coloured ribbons were fastened to their coats.

We looked on apprehensively, sensing the enormous power of these barely tamed animals, fearful that they might resist. Only a few days earlier, I had been a witness to the violent struggle between the nuns and the goats in Julichang. This time it was different – the monastery was in charge and the crisis of transition, associated with the change from one year to the next, slowly receded as each hour passed.

Memi Nasten retired to the temple with the rest of the monks and began the ceremony which would lead to the communal meal. The villagers relaxed and broke into loud cheers. Their jovial good humour burst out, and laughter and excited chatter ran through the monastery. Without waiting to be called by the bursar, the nuns hurried back to the kitchen. I was left alone with the village women.

They crowded around me, their bodies pressing closely against mine; rows of curious eyes met my awkward gaze. The children tugged at my clothes and, unable to resist the temptation, they ran their slight fingers over my shiny jacket. Suddenly I felt afraid. A chilling sensation of self-loathing swept over me. In an instant I was caught in its tight grip. My journey to Leh, the unresolved question of permission, the possibility of arrest, the sense of deception – all this flooded back into my mind. I could not look at the Yangthang women, at their open, smiling faces. Disentangling myself from their hold, I fled to the kitchen. The smell of cooked food filled me with nausea; but the nuns were too preoccupied to pay much attention to my abrupt appearance. I felt shaken and exposed, and I was grateful for the dim, smoky atmosphere of the interior. It protected me from quizzical glances and excused my restless movement about the room.

I tried to escape from the tyranny of my conscience by immersing myself in the bustling activity around me. There was little choice anyway, since the villagers had begun to assemble in the temple and the bursar arrived to oversee the serving of food. He put me in charge of the stack of plates which stood by the stove; and I passed them, one by one, to the nuns who ladelled out the contents of the great iron pots. The portions of steaming food, rice, and vegetables, were snatched from their hands by a succession of boys. Balancing as many plates as they dared, they bounded up and down the flights of stairs which linked the kitchen to the temple. It required skill and bravado not to miss a step or to be thrown off balance by their uneven surface. The boys, though, were cocksure and they delighted in frightening the bursar with their reckless confidence. It was their chance to express some of their youthful exuberance.

I kept pace with the others working in the kitchen; but we were caught up in an impersonal, mechanical routine. It increased my sense of dislocation. I felt remote, as if I were looking at a familiar scene which now seemed blurred and which shut me out. Soon we had only our own plates left to fill with food. The bursar departed and the nuns quickly pulled their robes into place. Sonam brushed my jacket and put her arm through mine. Quietly we entered the temple together.

The interior was dark, mysterious and cluttered once more. Rows of delicately painted silks hung low from the ceiling and adorned the walls. Each altar was covered with offerings, butter lamps, food, ceremonial scarves, incense, perfumes, and silks; and piles of sweet biscuits lay before the statue of the Buddha and the vacant thrones of Rizong's abbots. Even the receptacles from which tea was served were not those which were in everyday use, but highly polished brass and silver pots with exquisite filigree working.

The nuns took up their usual place behind the monks, while the villagers squatted on the floor at the side of the great doors. They ate noisily and the men maintained a lively conversation among themselves throughout the meal. Although the women were modest and reserved, there were hints of impatience at their confinement. The villagers could not begin their festivities until they had received Memi Nasten's blessing and a piece of the New Year offering. It seemed an interminable wait.

Eventually the villagers were called. Almost bent double, their rosary beads wrapped tightly around their cupped hands and bearing white ceremonial scarves, the men edged towards the senior monks. The women clustered together as a group, pushing their children ahead, anxious not to draw undue attention to themselves. Each villager offered a scarf to Memi Nasten and received it back from him with his blessing; and their outstretched hands accepted a portion of the offering.

I watched from the temple door with the nuns as we awaited our turn. I noticed Rigdol and Memi Nasten exchanging whispers and looking over to where I stood. To my surprise, I was summoned first. I hesitated and glanced uncertainly at the nuns; but the expression on their faces willed me forward. In the silence of that moment I knew that every pair of eyes in the temple had settled on me. I bowed low and offered my scarf. Memi Nasten leaned over and touched my head. At last I had received his sanction.

The villagers spilled out on to the balcony. They shook crumbs from the folds in their dress and began to pull on their boots. The pouches of the men's coats protruded. They were stuffed full of leftovers and pieces of the sweet biscuits handed to them by the monks as they left the temple. The women, in contrast, carefully preserved their appearance and carried the scraps in cloth bundles which dangled from their wrists.

I felt the villagers' scrutiny as I followed everyone outside. The nuns were delighted and Dondrup's face broke into a happy, toothless grin. A special blessing from Memi Nasten was unusual; and, temporarily, it assuaged my sense of guilt and drew me back into the heart of the community. I could now participate in the New Year celebrations with the confidence of Rizong's sanction and acceptance; but secretly I held on to each moment as if its passage brought me closer to what I believed to be an inevitable separation.

The musicians waited on the large open verandah beside the kitchen and they held their instruments at the ready. I was told that the men would open the dancing; and I found a place with everyone else at the edges of the arena while the monks gathered on the temple balcony above and vied with each other for the best view. With the steady beat of the drum setting the rhythm and a shrill pipe providing the melodic accompaniment, the men formed a circle and began to move in a clockwise direction. Their steps were slow and shuffling and they twisted, turned and bent their bodies in harmony with the music. The intricacy of movement lay in the interplay between the turn of their bodies and their elaborate hand gestures. Every aspect of the men's handsome appearance was enhanced by their graceful movement. Their New Year outfits were admired by us all – the finely woven wool of their coats and boots, the embroidered decoration, the dramatic contrast of the silk sashes tied around their waists and the stylishness of their brocade hats. Dancing in Ladakh was neither vigorous nor energetic; rather it was distinguished by its quiet elegance. It demanded poise, balance and co-ordination. Nordup possessed none of these skills. He declined to dance with the Yang-thang men and chose instead to stand on the periphery as a spectator with the goat man.

The women outmatched the men. Although the tempo and rhythm of dancing was the same for both sexes, they did not dance together but took it in turns to have the floor. As the women prepared to dance, I saw the change in their bearing and demeanour. Inside the temple they had been diffident and reserved: now they were confident again, almost majestic as they unashamedly displayed their beauty and adornment. The women knew they held our gaze as they moved slowly, their heavy jewellery clanking with every twist and turn; and they begged me to join them, promising to teach me the steps. Sonam pushed me forward and I was swept along in the line of women. The monks and nuns were greatly amused by my efforts. They were themselves forbidden by their Buddhist vows to participate in music or dancing; but this did not seem to deter them from following the villagers' activities with a keen and critical interest.

The young boys scurried around with pots of fresh tea and the goat man began to mingle with the spectators. His method was one of stealth. He would creep up behind unsuspecting monks, nuns or villagers and prod them sharply with his long stick. As his victims turned around, he pushed his mask close to their faces and erupted into peals of eerie high–pitched laughter. It was possible to escape from his grasp only by paying him a few rupees and accepting, for good fortune, one of the tiny goat effigies he kept in his front pouch. The goat man took delight in his ambiguity and the special powers he derived from the uncertainty of his status. He was half-human, half-animal; half male and half female – and he preyed on everyone.

During the afternoon the villagers dispersed and drifted in small bands around the monastery. The men took the opportunity to exchange news with the monks, and the women and children approached the bursar to request handfuls of walnuts and dried fruit. This was what he feared most of all. I gradually realized that the bursar's anxiety at New Year was not caused by the number of people for whom lunch had to be provided; but it stemmed from the threat of these visitors roaming the monastery, perhaps peeping into his storerooms, and making demands upon his carefully hoarded luxuries.

Reluctantly I left the dancing for the bursar's verandah and, with the nuns, I started to peel and core the vegetables for the days ahead. From our place on the terrace, we watched the annual battle unfold between the bursar and the village women.

The women from the Yangthang party grouped together outside Rizong's storerooms and began to ask for particular foodstuffs – initially their tone was polite; later it became mocking, almost threatening. The younger ones were restive and pushed forward to cluster around the bursar who stood guard with his arms outstretched across the doorway. He was easily outnumbered.

I saw him glance across to where we were sitting, but the nuns refused to acknowledge his implicit appeal for help. In an effort to placate the crowd, the bursar called to the young boys inside his rooms and instructed them to bring a small quantity of apricots and walnuts. They appeared, grinning slyly and wiping their mouths on their grubby sleeves. They obviously enjoyed the chance, like the villagers, to take liberties while the master's back was turned. This miserly gesture, however, only served to intensify the villagers' demands. The women began to jostle and to distract the bursar as their children wriggled and squeezed through the doorway to snatch handfuls from the open sacks.

I was sure that the bursar's resistance to their demands was not solely the result of his instinctive churlishness in sharing scarce foodstuffs. He was also determined to prevent the villagers from seeing the sheer quantity of these goods stored at the monastery.

The bursar was saved by the appearance of Memi Nasten on the balcony above. The women retreated quietly, pushing whatever they had managed to acquire, illicitly or otherwise, into their cloth bundles. The bursar could not be sure that he was safe; but he ran after the laughing villagers, shooing them off the verandah as if there had never been any doubt of his victory.

The light dimmed almost imperceptibly as the colourless winter afternoon merged with the encroaching dusk. A stiff breeze blew from the mountains and warned us of the night's advance. We had lost Nordup long ago; but from time to time we recognized his loud, raucous laughter above the music and general commotion. Now he appeared with four of the young village men to accompany us on the journey back to the nunnery. The youths were in high spirits and, slipping and sliding down the mountain path, they talked excitedly about the festivities which would continue after dark in Rizong's guest house and the next day at the nunnery. Tsodpah had been busy for weeks beforehand, brewing great quantities of beer and, with Nordup's help, she decanted a portion of it into several large clay pots. The nuns and I stood around with the men; they were eager to rejoin the Yangthang party and wasted no time in hoisting the brimming vessels on to their shoulders. Shrugging off their weight, they set off along the track, leaving the sound of their voices and laughter to hang in the valley long after they had vanished into the darkness.

We turned away from the entrance to Julichang and went inside – Sonam to the kitchen, the other nuns and me to the room off the courtyard where Tsering and Damchos had been waiting all day for our return. They were huddled close to a dying fire; and, although they felt the chill of the night as it closed in around them, neither of the women had the strength to revive the glowing embers. Samsten and Tsultim blew hard at the faint glow in the base of the fire. I pumped with the bellows. The pile of dry twigs was soon alight and tall, slender flames stretched towards the open chimney.

Dondrup came in from the animal sheds. She moved uncertainly, her body heavy with fatigue. She had checked that Rizong's herd had not broken loose during their confinement and now, having discharged her responsibilities for the day, she crept silently to her place in the corner. Tsodpah brought her a jug of beer and in no time at all, Dondrup was sound asleep.

The rest of us sat close to the fire and warmed ourselves with Sonam's tea. The nuns began to describe the temple ceremony at dawn. I watched Tsering and Damchos weigh every word as they recreated the brilliance of the scene in their imagination. It seemed so long ago that I found it difficult to believe it was a part of the time we still inhabited.

The thick air deadened all sounds from the mountain path and we did not hear the Yangthang party approach next day until it had almost reached the nunnery entrance. Its members were scattered. This time the women and children were the first to arrive; the men straggled far behind.

There had been no glimmer of sunlight for over a week, nothing but an impenetrable mass of grey cloud which seemed to sag lower in the sky as each day passed. The nuns watched the dark days with uneasiness. They felt the approach of snow in the damp air.

Winter in Ladakh was unrelenting; but there were variations

in the nature of its cold. The different sensations I experienced on my exposed skin alerted me to changes in the atmosphere. I perceived subtle shifts in our appearance and movement in certain conditions. Faces were always pale and angular in the dry cold of a clear, winter day; our movements were light, fluid and unrestricted in the great space which extended between earth and sky. In the thick, moist air of a sunless day it was different. Our faces became round and ruddy; we were slow and ungainly as if the weight of the dense cloud pressed down on every part of our bodies.

Despite a lack of sleep and the cramped, rudimentary conditions in Rizong's guest house, the splendour of the women's appearance remained undiminished. But I saw the softness in their beauty. At Rizong the day before it had been hidden behind the protective reserve they maintained in the presence of the monks. Now it seemed to fill their whole being. The nuns, too, seemed much less reticent, greeting the women affectionately and standing back to admire their fine costumes. They led them into a small room beside the summer kitchen and here, with their children, the women were served lunch.

There was a peaceful interlude before the village men approached the nunnery, their boisterous humour and deep lusty voices breaking through the heavy day. Tsodpah hurried out with jugs of beer and the other nuns peeped over the wall to see if the goat man was among the party. He was present, no less inscrutable than before and the ring of his odd, high-pitched voice was clearly audible above the general hubbub. He followed the men into Julichang and immediately cast around for unsuspecting victims. The nuns hid in the kitchen, but Tsering and Damchos were trapped and unable to escape.

Once the music started, the children crept into the courtyard to watch the dancing. They were no longer afraid of the goat man, and sensing the waning of his powers, they began to taunt him, pulling at his coat and mimicking his speech and shrill laugh. But the women did not join in the revelry. They wanted to retrieve their children because they were anxious to reach home before dusk and to make preparations for the imminent snowfall.

In the courtyard of Julichang, the afternoon dissolved in a haze of beer and steaming breath. The alcohol within the men burned deeply and it was expelled in the exertion of their movements. The men's spirits were unflagging; their dancing rhythm never faltered; and their wit and humour was irrepressible. In contrast, the goat man, his stick hanging limply at his side, sat apart, subdued, his potency spent.

At dusk the Yangthang villagers departed, taking with them all our New Year goat effigies. Later I found what I thought were dismembered dough scraps in the woodland at the side of the river.

Part Four
The Storm and After

Eighteen

The snow came. Dawn broke gently; but I felt a thin film of dew on my eyelashes and cheeks when I awoke. I opened the wooden shutters and looked out of the summer kitchen. Spirals of fine flakes floated and hovered in the leaden sky. Fleetingly, the columns appeared stationary, as if suspended in the rarefied mountain air. Their inertia was deceptive. Sudden gusts of wind blew through the valley, scattering the dry particles and creating dense snow flurries. In movement, the hard frosty edge of the flakes was whetted and they held little moisture to blunt the sting of their impact.

Beneath the window I saw several figures hurrying through the blizzard. Their heads were lowered, their bare arms exposed as they pulled threadbare robes tightly around themselves, shielding their bodies from the swirling splinters of ice.

I looked across the woodland to the solid rock walls of the valley which housed Julichang; but already the dark contours of our world had yielded to the storm and cut us free from the certainty of place. We were confined to the smoky winter workroom. It was not safe to venture any distance, even along the familiar river track to Rizong. The storm outside was reminiscent of a duststorm in its alternating calm and turmoil, in the speed with which fluctuations of movement obscured the landscape and induced a dangerous sense of dislocation.

The nuns, who at daybreak had battled against the storm, crouched close to the hearth. Their faces were red and chapped. They rubbed oil into their skin to relieve the painful smarting which came as the numb chill of their cheeks eased. In spite of the fire, the room was cold and draughty. The smoke rising to the open chimney had to battle with the wind outside and it was frequently forced back, filling the room and causing our eyes to prick with tears.

We took it in turns to look into the courtyard for signs of the storm's abatement. I planned to walk to Rizong with Tsultim and Samsten, since a village party from Hemis Shugba was expected in the late afternoon. We waited together through the dark, sullen morning. The nuns unwrapped the layers of oily, soot stained cloth which protected their scriptures and began to read. Such an opportunity came rarely to the women and they were unhurried, fingering and turning each page as if they felt its latent power.

We ate thin barley soup at midday, with the wind piercing every crevice in the walls and pushing down through the vent in the ceiling. Each icy blast forced us to edge closer to the fire. The nuns went on reading as if the storm shut out all other distractions; but its violence unnerved me. I felt uneasy.

Then, with an almost inaudible moan of exhaustion, the wind suddenly dropped and the last flurries of snow drifted to the ground. The afternoon became quiet; but the sky remained heavy and overcast. The nuns ventured out into the courtyard and carefully surveyed the clouds, assessing with an expert eye their shape, shade and movement. They did not anticipate another fall of snow until after dark. Tsultim, Samsten and I hastened to leave for Rizong.

Despite the ferocity of the morning's storm, it had left few traces on the ground. The particles of snow were so fine and dry that they merely formed a thin layer of dust which we kicked up like sand as we walked along the track beside the silent river. In places small drifts of light, powdery snow had been blown against the trunks of trees; and icy crystals clung to the bare branches. As we passed the woods, we disturbed foraging flocks of birds and they created great whirlwinds of tiny flakes as they scuttled across the frozen earth.

Rizong was silent. The monks had retreated with their scriptures into the lower levels of their cells to escape the biting wind. They remained hidden until the villagers came to pay their New Year respects. We made our way to the kitchen where we found the young boys, tired and miserable, huddled close to the stove. For once they had lost their sparkle; they looked bedraggled and forlorn, and their thin bodies shuddered with cold. The youngest boy sat apart, cowering in one of the dark corners. He had been crying and the others looked sheepish. The atmosphere suggested that they had pushed the bursar's patience too far with their pranks and that he had given them all a beating. The boys noticeably brightened at our appearance. The nuns spoke kindly to them and elicited with a smile the details of the morning's misdemeanours.

We could hear the bursar bustling about on the verandah above the kitchen. He had seen us arrive and he called down through the opening in the ceiling. Flinching, frightened of another explosion of anger, the boys jumped and hurried to stoke the fires; and we began to work our way through the usual tasks. The afternoon was gloomy and grey; and, in order to conserve our strength, we fell into a natural silence.

The light was already beginning to fade when the bursar dismissed us. I climbed the stony path ringing the monastery buildings and, with Tsultim, Samsten and the boys, I perched on a high narrow ledge which ran along the back of the temple. We looked out over unfamiliar territory. The juxtaposition of landscape and sky was unmediated by variations of light or shade. A uniform mass of grey cloud reached down to the frozen expanse of barren, black rock. The eye had no relief but the occasional movement of eagles, wheeling, turning and swooping between the different planes. It was easy to be deceived; and all kinds of shapes and silhouettes appeared out of the half-light only to dissolve as soon as the eye had fixed them in the landscape.

The Hemis Shugba party took us by surprise. The villagers crept noiselessly over the mountain range towards Rizong, unobserved until the last moment, when they were caught for a second as shadowy outlines on the sharp ridge which separated ground from sky. Then they plunged once more into the darkness and did not re-emerge as distinct figures until they stood before us in the twilight.

The older men, dignified and formal, carried long silver swords which hung from the gaily coloured sashes tied around their waists. The younger ones were haughty and unsmiling; and their tall, pointed black hats distorted the shape of their heads, giving them a sinister air. Accompanying the Hemis Shugba party were two musicians, a goat man and several horses, weighed down by bulging sacks of grain. No women, it seemed, had made the journey to the monastery.

The boys were thrilled by the villagers' attire and they skipped excitedly between the members of the party, whispering

loudly and imagining themselves to be fearless, heroic con-
quistadors. Even the goat man's powers seemed puny in com-
parison with this display. Instinctively feeling their way
through the warren of passages, the boys led the men down
from the mountain ledge and into the complex of buildings.
The villagers followed, groping in the thick, grey dusk, disoriented by sudden changes in direction and unsure of their footing on the uneven stone steps. We, too, were at the mercy of
the boys. The nuns were uncomfortable at being squeezed into
such a tight space with a crowd of unknown men. Their polite
reserve gave way to an awkward silence which did not lift even
when we emerged on to the open verandah below the temple.

The bursar hurried from his rooms to supervise the unloading of the horses. Heaving and struggling under their weight,
several of the young men carried the sacks of grain into the
temple as New Year offerings. The goat man lolled against
one of the great wooden doors and eyed us suspiciously; but
the other men, waiting by the entrance for the arrival of the
monks, had long forgotten our presence. I stood at a distance
with Samsten and Tsultim. We watched from the shadows as
the monks, alerted by the strains of music filling the chilly
night air, made their way in small groups to the temple balcony. They glided softly along the dark corridors, the sound
of their footfalls muffled by the thick woollen soles sewn to
the base of their winter boots. We heard greetings being
exchanged loudly with the villagers; but as the men filed into
the temple behind the monks, the noise and laughter of different voices gradually became indistinct. Finally, the great
wooden doors were pulled together, extinguishing the last
glimmer of light and leaving us outside, beneath a heavy,
moonless sky.

We set our faces against the biting wind and hugged the
ragged layers of cloth which covered us. They offered little
protection; the brutal edge of the wind bruised our bodies as
though we were naked. But walking down the path towards
Julichang, we smiled as the voice of an exasperated bursar followed us, ringing clearly through the frosty air. Soon his sharp
tones were muffled and faint, then inaudible. We turned the
first corner and descended quickly into the steep-sided valley.
Rizong disappeared behind us. For almost a week it existed
only in our memory.

Overnight the snow returned. Each day I looked out of the summer kitchen on to the unchanging scene, the single variation being the strength of the wind. The sudden squalls caused whirlwinds of icy particles to sweep across the landscape; the moments of stillness were filled with columns of fine, floating crystals. In those days our world shrank to the interior of the tiny workroom.

Nineteen

Damchos no longer ate breakfast with the nuns. At dawn Sonam went to her room with a bundle of twigs and dried cattle dung and quietly lit a fire while she slept. Later, I took her a small pot of soup from the kitchen. Flickers of light from the flames barely illuminated the room. When I entered I usually forgot to stoop and banged my head on the low ceiling as I stumbled in the half-darkness. Once my eyes had adjusted to the dim interior, I made out the shape of Damchos in the corner, lying beneath a pile of grimy rags. Here she slept with her inseparable companion, the cat. Damchos was virtually blind. For years her sight had steadily diminished until her eyes, watery and blank, stared unseeingly on to a dark, unfocused landscape. Her body was thin and frail and folds of dry, wrinkled skin hung from her wasted limbs.

Old age came early in Ladakh. The unforgiving climate and the strain of physical exertion at a high altitude resulted in premature ageing. The dry, desert air parched the skin, quickly robbing both men and women of their youth and vigour. I was, however, struck by the difference in appearance between the monks and the rest of the population. I had often looked closely into the faces of Rizong's inhabitants, intent on discerning evidence of spiritual distinction. In many cases I simply saw smooth, untroubled features; rarely, perhaps twice, had I glimpsed the stillness and serenity which marked profound religious devotion. I concluded that it was the absence of physical labour, rather than the depth of religious experience, which preserved the monks' appearance. The nuns, of course, were not spared the ravages of the climate; their features were coarsened, their skin creased and cracked, as a result of the years of unremitting outdoor work.

On hearing my clumsy footsteps, Damchos would call out for me to leave the pot on the hearth and she would enquire about the weather. It changed little, except to press in with each day's passing and hold us more tightly in its icy grip. Towards the middle of the morning, Damchos emerged, her head bowed and pushed forward as she fought against the driving swirls of snow. It was so big and heavy compared to her thin body and limbs, that it seemed almost to unbalance her as she gingerly felt her way across the courtyard to the workroom.

We listened for the tap of her stick and low voice calling to the cat. One of us, braving the cold, would step outside and guide her across the slippery stone flags to the workroom. The cat, never straying far from her side, darted in behind her. All day Damchos sat close to the fire; but she rarely broke into the chatter which surrounded her. She whispered prayers and counted rosary beads, her large opaque eyes gazing impassively ahead.

In the dark days of the storm, the nuns resumed the winter work disrupted by the New Year preparations and celebrations. Tsultim brought sacks of fleeces from the storeroom and emptied their contents across the floor. The wool had to be sorted, carded and spun. Spinning was a highly skilled operation learned by women in childhood. I watched with fascination the speed and agility with which the nuns carried out this process. They used finely chiselled wooden spindles, the point of one end placed in a moulded base made from the residue of the crushed apricot kernels. Attaching a fluffed-out section of the wool to the spindle, they spun it quickly, like a top, with their right hand, while the left hand held the carded wool and slowly drew it out. The two hands had to be closely synchronized if the thread was to be unbroken and even in its texture.

Once the spindle was full, it was passed to Tsering who wound the yarn into dense balls of thread. These were then hung from hooks in the walls and ceiling. She worked slowly but expertly; her hands were swollen and stiff with arthritis. Occasionally she was forced to stop as her joints seized up with cold, causing her to cry out in pain. Samsten began spinning after breakfast; later she was joined by Tsodpah and Sonam. Dondrup, Nordup and I, the unskilled labour force, worked at different tasks. We sorted the fleeces, teasing handfuls of wool from the mass, pulling the matted parts and loosening the knots in readiness for carding. This was Tsultim's job. She used a pair of heavy combs on the pieces we had sorted; and with several brisk, brushing movements she drew out the threads and created fine, fluffy wool which could be spun.

Nordup was usually the last person to settle himself to indoor winter work. After eating his morning soup, he went down to the animal sheds where Rizong's herd of sheep and goats was tethered. The animals were becoming increasingly boisterous and impatient during the long days of confinement. Sometimes Nordup received quite a mauling, being kicked and splattered with dung as he struggled to feed and secure them in the different compounds. We knew on his appearance in the doorway of the workroom if he had fought with the animals. He was breathless and untidy, his coat stained, his hat pushed to the back of his head, his great round face flushed and glistening with perspiration. Nordup viewed it as a test of his strength; and he relished recounting the details to us as he rested in the corner beside his jugs of beer.

He helped Dondrup and me with the sorting of the wool. Occasionally he did his own spinning; but the technique he employed was different from the one used by the nuns. It was not uncommon in Ladakh to see men take out a small wooden spindle from the front pouch of their coats and spin yarn while talking and drinking among themselves. The process the men used for spinning was simple and it required little speed or skill. The men also carried handfuls of carded wool during the winter months; and they could often be seen teasing it out, before attaching it to their spindles. The men's work was not a continuous, fluent activity, but rather halting and clumsy, since they could spin only short pieces of yarn at a time. For them spinning was a pastime, it was not the serious occupation it was for women in Ladakh.

One of Nordup's major tasks was to treat the skins removed from dead sheep and goats. Since the onset of the bitter cold, a number of Rizong's animals had been lost; either they had died in the sheds overnight or they had disappeared when roaming the mountainside during the day. Nordup always counted the herd at dusk and, if one member was missing, he would set out in the darkness, calling and whistling in an attempt to locate it. He was prepared to search the mountains and woods for hours rather than leave a weakened or dying animal to the mercy of the crows. The flocks of scavenging birds wasted no time, their eager hungry eyes quickly spotting a lone animal on the barren slopes. Then they would swoop and begin to pick at the warm flesh with their sharp, hooked beaks. Nordup listened in the darkness for the squawking and activity of crows overhead, for it usually directed him to the place on the mountainside where the carcass lay. He would sling the animal across his strong, square shoulders and bring it back to Julichang.

Nordup once explained to me that those animals which strayed several times were the ones he later found dead; it was as if, sensing the approach of death, they instinctively separated themselves from the rest of the flock. Nordup was protective of his animals. He took each loss seriously and reported it to the bursar.

It was Nordup's responsibility to skin the dead animals and this he did among the trees which ran down to the river. Although we never watched him execute the bloody task, we knew when it was being done as strange, almost wild, sounds would carry across the quiet air. The dog tethered by the entrance to the nunnery began to strain at its leash, to whine and howl excitedly as the scent of the meat reached its keen nostrils. After dismembering the body, Nordup would throw pieces of flesh to the dog. It pulled and tore greedily at them and played with the bones on the footpath for days. Nordup would skilfully remove the liver, intact, from the corpse and offer it to the nuns. Since the animal had died naturally and had not been killed, the eating of the meat was not strictly proscribed. Its status, though, was still ambivalent; and Nordup would never have dared to offer it to the monks for consumption. I felt slightly queasy at the prospect of eating the entrails of an animal which had lain dead on the mountainside for hours, picked over by carrion crows, before being found. But the nuns did not seem to be so squeamish. They cooked the liver with spices and butter and devoured it with obvious enjoyment. It offered a tasty respite from the thin grey soup we faced at every meal and which never satisfied our palate. The stodgy, brown dough served at lunch sank to the pits of our stomachs and gave a false sense of repletion. Occasionally, though, the tedium of the barley flour diet was enlivened by small portions of the spiced, oiled vegetables we had preserved and hidden from the bursar during the autumn; but the fresh ones, the turnips, carrots, and potatoes, had long ago been consumed. Each of us had been given sweet biscuits and dried fruit by the monastery at New Year and we tried as best we could to eke them out as the winter days stretched ahead.

Nordup soaked and cleaned the animal skins before he brought them into the winter workroom for oiling. His great calloused hands were cracked and swollen as a consequence of prolonged immersion in freezing water. As he rubbed and warmed them at the hearth, I noticed their red blotchy appearance and I wondered whether it was caused by the process of thawing or whether the patches were stains of dried blood. If it was the latter, Nordup would carry the blemish throughout the winter as every mark stubbornly clung to our rough, dry skins. We all steadily grew blacker. The smoke and soot from the fire became encrusted as a permanent layer on the exposed parts of our bodies. Washing in barely tepid water made little difference. The oil we rubbed into our weathered faces and hands merely deepened and fastened each stain.

The nuns were too busy with their spinning to assist Nordup in the treatment of the skins. They were also reluctant because they did not want their fingers to become greasy and spoil the fine quality of the yarn they spun. Nordup sought my help in kneading and softening the hides, a task which in the cold, arid atmosphere took many weeks to complete. First of all he showed me how to warm them over the fire, to stretch and massage them as the heat slowly infused the stiff, dehydrated skin. This opened the pores of the hide, increasing its suppleness and enabling the oil to be more readily absorbed. Nonetheless pressing the oil in was exhausting work. Generally we used butter; its distinctive rancid odour permeated the air and quickly became ingrained in our hands.

I worked in short bursts. Unused to such concentrated activity, my fingers ached; their tips became raw and tender owing to the friction generated by the rubbing of smooth oil into a coarse, parched texture. When I rested, I studied

Nordup's method. The strong ruddy hands moved almost without a pause, pulling, stretching, twisting and crumpling the hides. His fingers were short and fleshy and seemed out of proportion with the broad span of his hand. They were ragged too, the splintered, bitten-down nails clogged up with matted hair and dried blood. The roughness of his appearance, however, belied both his skill and his patient, gentle manner.

In the quietness of the workroom, Nordup's breathing was loud and laboured. Each exhalation inflated the big, round florid cheeks which nearly swallowed up all the other features of his face. He worked deftly, breaking the rhythm of movement only to snatch a gulp of beer or to push his hat back into its proper place on his head.

Watching Nordup, I detected the familiar dullness in his small deep-set eyes and the occasional lapses in concentration. I knew both to be indications of a temporary loss of bearings as he hovered between consciousness and sleep. In common with most of our work, the routine, the monotony of oiling the animal skins, and the constant whirring sound of the spindles, induced not exactly a state of drowsiness, but a kind of torpor. It was something we all tried to resist – disengagement, slipping away into a remote, disembodied world. The danger increased as we became marooned in the midst of the fierce storm which swept away our anchorage in the order and structure of the Himalayan landscape.

If Nordup caught sight of my interest, he blushed and a broad grin would stretch across his face to disguise his shyness. The old clumsiness often returned, and the clatter of his bowl or beer jug would cause the nuns to look up from their work and join in the friendly exchange between Nordup and me. But the chatter soon died down and we withdrew again into the work at hand. The pace was leisurely and we had no restless bursar to press and harry us. The room was silent but for the regular rise and fall of Nordup's rasping breath. From time to time the angry cry of the wind interrupted, rattling the door and pushing down the chimney, jolting us back into the bleakness of the winter's day.

Tsering was a renowned storyteller. Each day the nuns pestered her to relate the traditional narrative told in Ladakh after New Year. Often she did not respond, but lay throughout the morning beside the fire moaning, occasionally letting out a sharp cry, her body twisted and contorted with arthritic pain. Sometimes at night I heard her sobs carrying across the courtyard to the kitchen where Sonam and I were busy making butter. Sonam would wince and shake her head, helpless as we all were to do anything to relieve Tsering's condition.

The dark, cold days exacerbated her distress and the outbursts haunted the tiny room as an unsettling reminder of the painful inevitability of physical decay. At midday Samsten tried to coax Tsering and to persuade her to emerge from beneath the heavy blankets. I liked to listen to the sound of Samsten's voice; and I watched her as she gently rubbed Tsering's hands and promised her that the soup would help to warm and revive her stiffened limbs. Now and then it succeeded. Tsering's discomfort eased a little as the day passed and a keen sense of expectation became palpable. Like everyone else, I soon recognized the signs. When we resumed our work after lunch, we stole glances at Tsering, watching her prop herself up and rearrange the rugs over her gnarled limbs. The tension distorting her face lifted then and colour gradually seeped back into her cheeks.

Beginning softly, her low singsong voice drew us into the mythical world she created with words. It was inhabited by exotic creatures – snow leopards, yeti, eagles – all possessing magical powers, at times benign, at other times threatening and destructive. At the heart of the narrative was a long journey. We followed our hero as he moved between different worlds, through fragmented time, pitted against natural and supernatural forces. The tale was a sort of fable, weaving episodes of Ladakh's history with legends about the foundation and dissemination of Buddhism.

I often lost the thread of the story; but I was held by the sound of Tsering's voice and by those bright, luminous eyes which saw beyond the pain of her existence into strange, unfathomable regions.

Twenty

We turned our backs on the bitterness of the Himalayan winter and became absorbed in the life of the crowded workroom. No one remarked on the passage of time, for each day was as bleak as the one before. I too had to accept the season's cruelty; but its turbulence penetrated my consciousness, stirring up many of the doubts and uncertainties which I sought to repress. Often I looked around the workroom, seeking reassurance in a scene which now seemed so familiar; yet it eluded me, even when one of the women, sensing my quizzical gaze, looked up from her work and smiled silently at me. I found myself returning again and again to the New Year, recreating the different episodes in my mind in an attempt to locate the cause of my unease; but I was no longer certain that the images which I evoked were true reflections of what I had seen. I knew, though, that the period of transition had changed us all; and that it had laid bare the contradictions which fractured the lives of these servants of the Buddha as they struggled to find spiritual fulfillment.

Perhaps a week elapsed. We were resting in the middle of the morning when Samsten startled us by shouting and pointing excitedly to the vent in the ceiling. We looked up to see a shaft of weak sunlight just touching the edges of the chimney. She scrambled to her feet and hurried to pin back the door of the workroom, allowing the delicate light to spread through its thick, dingy interior. Tsering peeped out from under her blankets, blinking as she adjusted to the daylight, and Damchos turned towards the open door to feel the warmth upon her shrivelled face. But I went outside with Sonam, Tsultim, and Tsodpah to bask in the pale sunshine which bathed the courtyard. The sun was still low in the sky, barely peeping above the steep walls of the river valley. Its rays stretched down to the nunnery for less than an hour; then the yellow light faded and the heavy golden dome slipped from view, leaving only faint traces of its gentle warmth on our bodies. But every day the rays of sunlight penetrated deeper into the valley and lingered for a few moments longer on the cold surface of black rock walls.

When we finished our midday meal and returned to the tasks around the hearth, I noticed that we had relaxed and let slip the instinctive gestures which had helped to shield us from the wind's savage blows. We no longer crouched defensively over the fire or stooped under the weight of a sagging sky. The door of the workroom was open and the air felt cool and light. Tsering slept. Her twisted body was still, and in repose her breath ebbed and flowed with low, easy sighs. For the last few days she had been caught up in the turmoil of the storm, her vulnerability exposed as she was tossed by its fickle, restless moods, bound in moments when it subsided to its quiet unbending will. It seemed to have taken all her strength to resist its power and now she lay exhausted. The nuns were protective of her and watched carefully over every movement of her slight frame as they worked.

The peace of the winter afternoon was eventually broken by the furious barking of the dog. We looked across at one another and smiled. A moment later the bursar was standing before us in the doorway of the workroom. Behind him limped the boys, each of them struggling with bulky sacks which kept slipping off their thin, bony shoulders and bumping awkwardly against their legs. Their faces were pinched and sallow, almost ghostly, as if life had drained away during their days of confinement within the monastery. We probably looked the same. I had long ago lost any sense of how I might appear to anyone else. It had not occurred to me to carry a mirror in my luggage. The only time I caught a glimpse of my face was when the sun reflected on the single pane of cracked glass in the window of the summer kitchen. In the winter this was a rare event and I quickly forgot the details of my external persona. I knew, however, that the sensations internal to my body found expression outside; and, when I ran my fingers over my skin, it often felt shrivelled and bloodless, sometimes fiery and stinging. There seemed to be no comfortable equilibrium: either my face was taut and numb, or it burned and the hot blood pulsed through my veins.

The bursar had brought bundles of fleeces from his storeroom for the nuns to card and spin. Given the capriciousness of the winter weather, he was not going to take any chances with supplies. He preferred to burden us with too much work rather than run the risk of idle time at Julichang.

Settling himself beside the fire with the boys, the bursar began to talk about the storm.

As the snow swept over the mountains, the monks had sought refuge in the lower parts of their cells. The balconies above, where they usually sat during the day, were open to the elements and the wind rushed in, tossing and scattering flakes across the uneven flagged floors. The monks listened to the changing sounds of the wind, waiting for its angry bluster overhead to give way to a distant muted roar. Then cautiously they emerged from the enclosed lower recesses and brushed away the covering of powdery snow from the open balconies. Light streaked across the sky; the monks seized these precious moments to escape the unchanging blackness below.

The bursar began to speak with animation, unable to contain the boyish excitement of being swept along by the turbulence of the storm. It kept breaking through in his rapid, breathless speech and in his energetic gesticulations. Without being aware of it, he shed the gruff impatience he displayed in his routine dealings with the nuns, and the sharp angles of his elongated face relaxed to reveal youthful impetuosity.

It was clear that the monks had experienced a different sort of dislocation during the climatic upheaval, one which filled them with a feeling of exhilaration, almost cathartic in its intensity. This partly stemmed from the altitude and position of the monastery within the dry, pitted landscape. Rizong was built into a sheer rock face high above the narrow river valley. Its situation conveyed a dizzying sense of height, opening up an unlimited range and depth of vision we never knew at Julichang. In contrast to our sense of powerlessness as we lay beneath a massive sky, alternately buffeted and suspended by the wind's fickle moods, the monks had at times looked out from their balconies directly into the eye of the storm. The world below them vanished and they were carried high into the clouds, moving through the shifting patterns of light and dark as they were drawn ever closer to its vortex. The monks felt a tremendous surge of power.

We knew its residue still clung to the bursar; and no one dared break the spell the storm cast over him as he relived its force and ferment. Eventually he lapsed into silence. The nuns looked away and returned to their work. There was a defensiveness in their manner when they bent stiffly over the spindles and began pulling at the thread. I felt it too. The bursar had reawakened memories of the fragility of our lives during the storm.

In a characteristic gesture, revealing his awkwardness, the bursar shrugged his shoulders and growled at the boys. They shrank back, watching him nervously; but the nuns continued to bend low over their work and refused to meet his eye. He turned to address me and, for a second, I saw a hint of cruelty in his pinched, angular face. The pale skin was stretched tightly, mask-like, over the sharp features and the flush of excitement which earlier had softened his appearance had left no mark on this cold, seamless exterior. His face looked very long and narrow, the smooth facade crosscut by a thin mouth twisted into an unpleasant sneer.

I was uncomfortable to be the sole object of his scrutiny. I heard the flat monotone of his voice disturbing the stillness of the fading afternoon, but I was unable to focus properly on what he was saying. His words sounded harsh and loud, almost distorted; and, as vessels of the storm's residual power, they fell like blunt instruments on the thin air. The nuns withdrew in order to protect themselves. Likewise, Dondrup and Nordup remained silent, their faces set and closed as they looked steadily into the fire.

The bursar prepared to leave, taking out from a cloth bundle supplies of candles and kerosene which he gave us to enable our work to continue after nightfall.

We listened for the dog's angry barking to subside, knowing then that the bursar and the boys had passed into the woods and that we lay beyond their reach. Dusk was drawing in. Samsten went to close the door on the breeze which was beginning to whip up fine drifts of blown snow lying across the courtyard.

The evenings stretched out ahead of us.

Twenty-One

The days were cold and cloudless, and we moved freely outside as if a leaden weight had been lifted from our limbs. We
had become accustomed to the thick, muffling cloud; but now
we laughed as we heard our voices ringing through the light,
clear air. We played games with sound, calling to one another
and listening to the words expand, vibrate and echo between
the rock walls of our valley. But at the back of our minds
lurked the fear of suffocation by the dense silent blizzards. We
remembered our physical vulnerability in the face of the brutal
icy winds which tore through the deep gorge housing Julichang. The atmosphere in which we worked had been changed
too by the storm; and the threat of its return hung over us. We
could never be sure when its violence would again shake the
foundations of our world. These moments of exuberance were
brief and rare. Our unspoken apprehension drew us together;
but the winter made us introverted and the private space each
of us inhabited remained, despite the rigid confines of our daily
lives. Often I remembered the early days of summer and
autumn when, shortly after dawn, the nuns would scatter and
disappear for the day into the woods, orchards, and fields.
Although the women returned tired and limping at dusk, their
faces were open and glowing; but now they sat hunched before
the fire, their limbs cramped and unused. The nuns rarely
strayed beyond the courtyard and only snatched moments of
outdoor solitude, as though they feared it. The smoky workroom became their refuge in an uncertain world.

Shafts of pale sunshine broke through the valley at midday
and tempered the chill of the frosty air. I sat outside with Tsultim and Tsodpah, quietly soaking up the delicate warmth,
breathing deeply in an effort to expunge the dust and soot
which clogged our throats and lungs. For days I had tasted
nothing but woodsmoke in my dry mouth; and its stale, pungent odour permeating my body gave me twinges of nausea. In
the daylight I noticed that the nuns looked odd; their faces were
slightly shrunken and drained of colour. The pallor of their
skin was reminiscent of a long sickness. We were all ragged
and grubby. The fleas had become restless, moving about in

our seams as the warmth and light penetrated the layers of tattered cloth. One or two of the nuns jumped up and down, shaking their clothes; but still the fleas clung tenaciously to our soft, moist flesh.

Nordup was absent. In the early morning, with noise and commotion, he had herded the sheep and goats out along the river track. I had watched him depart from behind the high nunnery wall, his hot, steamy breath rising as he gulped great mouthfuls of clean air. He was surrounded by an impatient flock. The animals pushed and butted him; but he ignored their boisterous attack with equable humour. He relished the prospect of a day outdoors, alone, roaming through the mountains with a large piece of beer-soaked dough in the front pouch of his coat.

Some time later Dondrup appeared, grumbling to herself, shuffling slowly as she shooed the cattle ahead of her. They were quick to spread out and, with their noses pressed to the ground, they headed off into the woods, searching for fodder between the drifts of snow and the exposed patches of barren soil. By the afternoon I feared that the cattle would be on the screes which stretched up to the skyline behind the monastery; and I left soon after lunch to retrieve them. Although there were still several hours of daylight, I wanted to give myself plenty of time before dusk fell. I had not climbed the steep stony path to Rizong for many days and I knew the effects of the altitude would be debilitating.

I walked slowly through the woods, following the tracks of tiny hoof prints left by the sheep and goats as they passed over the fine powdery snow covering the path. In places, deep drifts were strewn across the way and I scrambled over the hard, tightly packed ice by stepping into the large depressions left by Nordup's flat feet. Breathless, my legs weak and heavy, I finally emerged out of the cold, shadowy valley from where the rays of sun had long since faded; and I entered a band of brilliant sunshine which bathed the higher mountain slopes. Here I rested against a pile of rocks and, soothed by the warm golden light, I closed my eyes.

Turning the last corner, Rizong came into view. I found myself looking objectively at the stack of whitewashed buildings as if I was approaching the monastery for the first time. Barely a week had passed since I was last there with the nuns

at New Year; but the storm violently intruded, its force lingering in my subconscious, rupturing the continuity of memory.

I felt detached and a little uneasy as I climbed the last stretch
of the path which led into Rizong. But suddenly the sound of
Rigdol's booming voice came out of the silent, deserted maze
of cells and startled me. My sessions with him had never settled
into a regular pattern. For a month or more, he had been a
distant, formal figure, preoccupied with the rituals of New
Year; and I, in common with the nuns, had been in awe of
him, sensing the weight of his learning and the depth of his
spiritual power. With some trepidation, I made my way to his
room; but he welcomed me in a kindly way, ushering me to a
place on the balcony beside his table of texts and close to a
small pile of glowing embers which warmed a pot of butter
tea. He enquired after the nuns. He was anxious about the
harshness of winter life at Julichang and he asked me if I found
conditions difficult and oppressive. Rigdol never once referred
directly to the storm.

I listened to the melody of his soft voice, its calm, measured
tempo; but there was a trace of weariness in the distinctive
tones. I looked again in Rigdol's face. I saw none of the obdu-
racy of the bursar or the chilly disdain of Memi Nasten; but I
saw that the period of intense ceremonial activity had marked
him. He was pale and tired.

Rigdol unwrapped one of the texts and handed it to me in
unbound cloth. I sat cross-legged beside him and, spreading
the silk brocade across my lap, I carefully arranged the pages
for reading. Religious texts were always handled with the
utmost care. To drop them on the floor or to place them in
contact with grimy, everyday surfaces constituted a serious
transgression.

I turned the first page. Instinctively I imitated the nuns' habit
when they found a moment for prayer after the day's work
was over and I ran my fingers over the rough parchment
leaves, feeling the imprint of the thick, black letters pressed
into the paper. Scriptures were not merely the repositories of
the wisdom and teaching of the Buddha; as objects they were
deeply imbued with mystical power. Many weeks had elapsed
since I had last studied with Rigdol; and, although I could read
the Tibetan script, I had earlier struggled to find the fluency of
recitation necessary to free the words from their boundary in

the text. The act of reading was rarely a silent event, even when the monks were alone in their cells, since the articulation of sound and the resonance of the words opened up different layers of consciousness as the prelude to meditation.

The text I was given on this occasion by Rigdol contained prayers and offerings to Dolma. She was much revered and her compassionate qualities made her one of the most popular deities in the Tibetan Buddhist pantheon. Invocations to Dolma were permanently on the lips of both monastic and lay devotees; and, without being fully aware of it, I had absorbed these sounds, and the rhythm of words and phrases had become lodged in my mind.

I started hesitantly. At first the rows of smudged print appeared strange and impenetrable; but I listened to the deep, steady tone of Rigdol's voice filling the uncertain pauses. Then the words began to spill out. The sonority of the cadences, the gentle rise and fall of sound filled my whole being. I merged into the rhythmic chant which encircled me.

We came to the end of the text. Our voices ceased; but the echoes lingered and slowly died away in the valley beneath us. The air felt soft and still on my cheeks. I closed the text and folded the heavy cloth over the fragile paper. Shyly, I handed it to Rigdol. He smiled and, for a moment as his face creased, the strain and weariness clouding his features lifted. Then he turned back to the texts and he became again the remote figure I could only glimpse with the nuns from our place at the margins of the temple.

I crept from the room and made my way along the empty passages to the kitchen. The boys told me that the bursar was busy helping the doctor make medicines, and one of them offered to take me to the room where they were working. I followed him and found myself straying once more into the hidden recesses of the monastery. We seemed to be heading down a long tunnel which grew darker with every step; but eventually, after turning yet another tight corner, the boy paused and began to fumble loudly with a heavy iron clasp in the wall. Perhaps the door was difficult to open or perhaps he was deliberately making noise to warn the men of our approach. I did not know; but, using his shoulder to give the door a hefty shove, the boy pushed it open and we came out into a light, spacious hall. He whispered to me that we were entering Rizong's debating chamber. It was used only when one of the abbots was in residence at the monastery.

I imagined it packed with eager, excited monks; their voices shrill and penetrating, questions and responses to points of Buddhist doctrine ranging back and forth, punctuated by the characteristic smack of the hands which marked every challenge. A year earlier in Dharmsala, when walking in the woods beneath the Dalai Lama's palace, I had occasionally stumbled across open-air debates held in the nearby monastery courtyards. I would be alerted by the sound of raised voices separated by a sharp crack which broke through the dormancy of the heavy, damp Himalayan days. These debates were always an impressive display of intellectual versatility and verbal fluency; and I was quickly lost in the intricate maze of philosophical exposition. But now it was different. I was no longer awed by monastic scholarship. The claims of the monks to be the true guardians of the faith jarred with my experience of the simple spiritual dignity with which the women at Julichang lived their lives.

As I stood in the doorway of Rizong's debating chamber, I sensed a chill of desolation which reminded me of the abbot's empty suite and meditation room hidden elsewhere in the monastery. The high walls, smooth and white, the flat, earth floor, the tall windows stretching almost to the ceiling through which filtered the pale afternoon light, accentuated the proportions. In the middle of this bare, cavernous room and surrounded by medicinal ingredients sat the bursar and the doctor. It seemed strange to see the bursar on his hands and knees, meekly obeying the doctor's curt orders and deferring to his expertise as he groped among the dried leaves scattered over the dirt floor. He looked relieved at my appearance and immediately delegated the searching to me, while he dusted down his crumpled robes and hurried to inspect the line of polished pots in which the ingredients would be combined.

There was an air of urgency to the work. Everything had to be ready by dusk when Rigdol would arrive to supervise the making of the medicine. It was something I would not be allowed to witness, partly because it would take place after nightfall and partly because it was a ceremony full of esoteric practice. The doctor told me that the transformation of the herbs and minerals into a potent substance would act as a protection against the rigours of the Himalayan winter and ward off the dangers of sickness in the year to come.

I feared most for Damchos and Tsering. Their frail wasted bodies seemed barely to contain life; but I had also discerned strain and uncertainty in the faces of all Rizong's monks and nuns. The realization of their vulnerability disturbed me. Although I did not dwell on it, I was conscious of a fear tightening in my stomach. I felt afraid of what lay ahead.

Twenty-Two

Suddenly I noticed the darkening sky. The herd of cattle were high above the monastery, strung out across the scree; but the animals showed no signs of preparing to descend. Reluctantly I started to scramble up the sheet of loose rocks, cautiously edging towards them. It was a slow, punishing climb demanding both balance and stamina. With each step I struggled to find a secure foothold; but my advance was frequently checked by sliding stones which pushed me back several yards down the scree. My fear was that the movement of the cattle over the slopes combined with the disturbance I created might dislodge one of the large, heavy rocks perched closed to the ridge. In the near darkness I probably would not see it tumble down the slope until it was virtually on top of me. Even if I managed to avoid being struck, there would be nothing to check the rock's gathering momentum as it hurtled dangerously towards the monastery buildings at the foot of the scree.

I hoped my approach would stir the animals, but they ignored my shouts, shrugging off the small pebbles I threw at them and continuing to press their noses to the ground as they rummaged among the dry rocks. After many days tethered indoors I knew they were going to be obstinate. I climbed higher until I was close to the upper ridge; but, in concentrating on the stones immediately before me, I was unaware of the speed with which the light was fading from the evening sky. Once I was above and behind the line of cattle, I stopped and rested. I sat down on the rough, shifting stones and looked below. Dusk had dissolved the landscape, merging it into the dark sky; and an expanse of greyness surrounded me. I listened to the cattle. The animals were sure-footed and bold; they clattered down the sheer slope, heading by instinct for the familiar path to Julichang. I envied their fearlessness. The prospect of descent was daunting, but I could not delay. The cows were already ahead of me and, given their recalcitrance, there was every danger they would not stay together as a herd, but separate in the darkness. A night in the mountains at this time of year would probably be fatal; and I dared not consider the prospect of Nordup searching the slopes the next day for a frozen carcass.

I began to pick my way gingerly across the scree, crouching close to the ground, conscious all the time of the strong pull downward. I had to resist the urge to follow the cattle, to give in to the desire to plunge helter-skelter down the treacherous slope in an effort to break the unbearable tension wound tightly around my body. I held back and embarked on a hesitant decline. I left behind the sharp outline of crags which marked the summit and, until I was able to make out the shape of the monastery below, I was in limbo, suspended in a noiseless grey void. Step by step I navigated a zigzagging route. I caught my breath each time a foothold gave way beneath me, upsetting my balance and causing a sudden rush of stones down the mountainside. Every part of my body was taut and the muscles in my legs burned. As Rizong came into sight, I relaxed and immediately I half-slid, half-tumbled down the last few feet to the bottom of the scree. I could no longer sustain the concentration and control that the steep descent had demanded and my legs buckled weakly. I lay against the cold rocks, dazed and breathless, listening to the sound of my heart racing from a mixture of exertion and relief.

From somewhere in the monastery, one of the boys called out to me. He had heard the noise of moving stones and he was afraid that I had been swept down the slopes in a rockfall. I shouted back through the darkness and, getting shakily to my feet, I prepared to continue the journey home. First of all I had to find the cattle.

The boy approached me as I brushed the dry earth from my clothes. He explained to me that he had caught and secured the animals in one of the compounds below the monastery. I filled his hands with walnuts and dried apricots given to me over the New Year by the bursar; and I set off down the mountain track, herding the cattle in front of me.

Usually I returned to the nunnery at dusk when the last glimmer of light cast strange shadows across my way; but the gloaming had long since gone. Darkness cloaked the landscape and the night sky was heavy and black. The animals bunched together on the path, jostling for the middle ground, their wilfulness tempered by the gloom which pressed in on every side. I kept close to them and, although I knew the path almost stone by stone in the daylight, I sought comfort in the herd's instinct for home. We passed into the steep, twisting corridor which linked Rizong with the river valley, the woods and Julichang below. The breeze dropped and the night became hushed and still. It was airless between the high rock walls and my breath quickened.

Twenty-Three

The darkness was eerie. Lacunae appeared in the night canopy as clouds slid overhead and allowed glints of silvery moonlight to filter through, catching different facets of the valley sides. The contours of the rock walls were not fixed and immutable as in the harsh brightness of day. Night revealed the deceptiveness of form, uncovering lines of deposit and erosion in the rugged, weathered texture of the landscape.

As I walked, phrases from the scripture I had been reading with Rigdol reverberated through my head. It was impossible to remember all the words; but I knew their sound and movement; I sensed the power which lay somewhere beyond their meaning and was generated in the rhythm of recitation. I feared losing my hold on the words, for their resonance and the elusive spatial dimensions of the valley threatened to estrange me from the surrounding world.

In this deep gorge I experienced a terrifying moment of suspension when the solidity of the landscape appeared illusory. Until then I had accepted that the order of the community was closely tied to the natural features of our world, our work defined by the regularity of the climate, seasons, terrain; our perspective secured within the lines of the valleys and mountains. But suddenly the structure and routine of nunnery life, which I believed to be built into the Himalayan range, seemed to have dissolved in my grasp; and I knew I could not again capture that sense of order and stability which I once thought anchored our lives at Julichang. Earlier I had sensed apprehension and caught glimpses of vulnerability in the faces of the nuns, occasionally in those of the monks. Now I understood our fragility as we perched precariously in the midst of this hideous, dominating Himalayan mass. When the nuns flinched at the prospect of winter, they were not just bracing themselves for climatic severity; rather the gesture betrayed their fear of having to draw on great reserves of strength in order to resist the force and irruption of the landscape into their lives.

Eventually I reached the fork in the path. The cattle increased their pace as they turned the corner for home; but I dropped behind, shaken and preoccupied with the surge of impressions which had emerged in the shifting half-light of the gorge. The voices of Dondrup and Sonam broke into my brooding introspection. I heard them calling to each other as they counted the cattle emerging from the woodland within sight of the nunnery. It was late and our absence beyond dusk had begun to cause anxiety. I cursed my own carelessness: so absorbed had I become in my own tangled thoughts and fears that one of the animals could easily have strayed into the woods without my noticing it. I would not even have been able to tell Nordup where on the track it had disappeared.

As I made out the familiar whitewashed walls of Julichang, I had a strong sense of approaching home; but at the same time I was aware that my relief was mixed with twinges of apprehension. I was sure that I looked different, that somehow my appearance had changed during my descent from Rizong and that the turmoil in my mind would be clear for everyone to see.

Sonam had gone ahead to fasten the animals in the compound, but Dondrup remained behind, waiting for me beside the nunnery entrance. I knew from her open, creased face that all the animals had returned safely; and, as I reached her, she smiled and affectionately pressed my arm. I felt awkward and turned to go into the dark kitchen where I could be alone with Sonam. She was my close companion and on many evenings, when we crouched over the dying embers of the fire, she sang Ladakhi songs for me. Their haunting, nostalgic tone was a link to her childhood and to the household life she had left behind as a young girl, barely six years old. Unlike many of the other nuns at Julichang, Sonam was not from one of the nearby settlements, but from a tiny village on the outskirts of Leh. The day of her arrival at the nunnery had left an indelible impression upon her and, of course, the memory she retained was that of a child in its vividness and intensity, recalling her sense of bewilderment at the dimensions of the world opening up before her.

Sonam's early years were dominated by the sickness of her mother. The strain of successive pregnancies had weakened her and she began to suffer periodic bouts of fever and delirium. One winter her mother's condition worsened. Weeks passed without her being able to leave her bed. Her skin became sallow and wrinkled, her eyes dull, sinking deeper into the bony cheeks, as each day Sonam watched the ebbing of her strength. The family consulted a number of learned monks; and different healing rituals, often lasting several days at a time, were performed in the household by monks from one of the local monasteries.

Sonam remembered the bustle and activity surrounding each occasion: the preparation of a room for the ceremony, the cleaning and polishing of household utensils, the cooking of special foods, the deferential whispering and tiptoeing as they tried to carry out the routine domestic tasks without disturbing the concentration of the monks closeted away with their texts and ritual paraphernalia. But it was the strange sounds interrupting their lives, the unbroken chant like a long, deep growl and the sudden bursts of music echoing through every part of the house, which filled Sonam's childhood memories.

She told me how she would listen for the climax in the ceremony, when the monks' voices were raised, almost angry, and the discordant, jarring tone of the drums, cymbals, horns, and bells reached a deafening crescendo. At that moment everyone in the house became silent; they listened intently for the door to creak open and for one of the monks to hurry outside with the dough offering. They all shrank back until it was safely removed from the house and then a sense of relief began to settle over everyone as they returned to their work. But Sonam would peep through the wooden shutters and watch the monks throw the offerings into the scrubland which ringed the village. They were polluted and they lay untouched, until they were discovered and devoured by roaming dogs or hungry crows. Slowly the tension in the household eased and the noise from the monks' room subsided into a soft rhythmic chant.

Gradually Sonam's mother gained strength. On recovery she resolved to offer her second daughter to the Buddhist faith. Nunneries were scarce in the Himalayas and she sought the advice of one of Ladakh's leading abbots. He suggested the small community of nuns attached to Rizong monastery, since it was a foundation widely renowned for its scholarship, discipline and integrity.

Sonam and her mother set out for Julichang at the end of winter. They travelled for days on horseback, spending their nights resting and feeding their animals in different villages along the way. They were journeying from their home to a place they considered to be a foreign country. But it was not the long, tiring days crossing the rocky terrain which Sonam recalled, but the final leg, the approach to Julichang.

She recounted it in a whisper and I watched her closely as the changing expressions on her face betrayed the complexity of the memories. It was early spring. There was a touch of frost in the air, but the sky was clear and the sun had begun to melt the layers of snow and ice deposited during the long winter months. The river was fast-flowing and, as the thick crust cracked and broke up, clumps of ice floated in the swollen waters. Sonam and her mother followed its course and began their long walk into the mountains. They left behind the wide, sunny plains and open valleys of Sonam's childhood and began to penetrate deep into the narrow, craggy gorge. To her child's eye, the tall black walls enclosing the valley towered menacingly over Sonam: and she had felt afraid as the dusty track seemed to stretch endlessly ahead until it merged into the grey landscape. The sun was directly overhead, its rays gentle and warming; but the glare almost blinded the weary travellers. The valley offered no shade or protection from the fierce light and, in places, pools of still water reflected the brilliance of a cloudless azure sky. Sonam unconsciously screwed up her eyes, wrinkling and distorting her face as she relived the fatigue, the thirst, the mixture of uncertainty and adventure which marked her approach to the nunnery.

I was drawn easily into the narrative, caught by the intensity and poignancy of Sonam's emotions and by the stark evocation of a scene which echoed my own journey to Julichang. Sonam related the story to me several times and I learned to anticipate the moment in her account when, slightly breathless, she paused. Then her face softened. In a whisper, her eyes wide and bright like a child's, she recalled how abruptly the landscape changed, as the travellers, emerging from a series of twists in the track, suddenly saw a dark cluster of vegetation ahead. The tension gave way to excitement and laughter as the terror of the deep, dry valley was broken by evidence of human settlement and cultivation.

The narrow path straightened and its gentle slope led higher, drawing them away from the river's edge until the sound of water in the valley below became muted, muffled by the terraces of woodland which stretched down to the bank. Sonam and her mother entered the cool, shady tunnel of green trees. Here they rested on a bed of dry leaves and grey earth; the new, heavy foliage had not yet been parched and shrivelled by the sun and it shielded them from the intense brightness of the spring day. Her mother was pale and exhausted; but Sonam was restless, curious to see Julichang and to catch sight of the women about whom curious tales were told. They splashed their faces and hands with icy water from the river and made ready for their arrival.

As they came within sight of the nunnery, the dog startled them. It sprang from its kennel and, pulling at its leash, began to bark wildly. The noise shattered the silence of the valley. Moments later two nuns peeped over the high wall and beckoned them inside. Sonam's excitement had vanished. She was fearful and she clung tightly to her mother as they walked into the open courtyard.

They spent most of the summer together, working in the fields and orchards with the nuns; but as autumn approach Sonam's mother prepared to return to her home village. Sonam remembered the tears she had shed as she watched her mother disappear down the long, dusty track. The departure closed the door on her childhood, severing her links with household and village life. It became another world, hidden; one to which Sonam returned only silently in her dreams and memories.

I was always intrigued when I caught glimpses of the women's pasts; they were rare and fragmented, vivid, snatches of individual experience buried deep beneath the routine of everyday life. Despite the sharing and co-operation between the nuns in the tasks which filled their days, the irksome demands of the bursar, the constraints of the annual cycle of work – despite all this, I still found myself drawn back to the moments in which I perceived a gap, a disjunction, between the order and monotony of communal life and their existence as isolated, individual women. The nuns never spoke of their communal history, since it was unchanging and embedded in the structure of work which so tightly circumscribed their lives. But each of them clung to something else which they did not share, rooted as it was in their unique and separate existences.

I often thought about Sonam's arrival at the nunnery, turning over in my mind the details, the changing expressions in her voice and face as she cautiously tunnelled a way into her past. Like the other nuns at Julichang, she preserved an area of private space, the kitchen; but over the winter months I had been slowly drawn into her solitude. In the long hours of darkness we inhabited a different place. At night Sonam never spoke of the other nuns, she retreated from that life into an amorphous, highly personal, individual world.

The conversations I had with Sonam in the kitchen forged a bond between us. It was symbolized in our common journey to Julichang, a journey we recreated as a means of reaching beyond the confines of monastic life into a silent well of memory. But, if the walk through the narrow valley provided the link between us and between our separate and communal lives, I knew too that the same dusty track divided us. It was my route back into the world outside.

I waited in the dim, smoky kitchen for Sonam to finish milking and feeding the cattle. I dwelled on the prospect of my departure from Julichang. Increasingly it haunted me, as if the climatic upheaval had posed anew the question of my place in this Himalayan community. In the immediate aftermath of the storm I felt troubled and unsettled, conscious of a shift in my perception of the nuns; and, in the half-light of dusk on the mountains above Rizong, I realized that something fundamental, but personal to me, had occurred. I had penetrated beneath the surface, below the pragmatic structures, the rootedness of nunnery life; and, straying into hidden recesses, I had discovered the fluid, fragile nature of its foundations. I could no longer escape the knowledge of the women's fractured lives, the scars laid bare in a brutal, unforgiving climate. Now I felt I was compelled to decide: either I had to become part of that life, submitting to the violence and the uncertainty, accepting its wounds and fissures, or I had to cut myself free, through withdrawal and departure.

I heard Sonam's light footsteps outside and the low hum of her voice, murmuring an unbroken stream of prayers under her breath. She appeared in the doorway of the kitchen with two pails of milk and, squinting as the acrid smoke pricked her eyes, she grinned when she saw me struggling to stoke a dwindling fire. Gratefully I exchanged places with Sonam; her expert way with the bellows cleared the kitchen in no time and she hurried to assemble the churn and whisk for buttermaking. Instead of the usual leisurely pace which characterized the time we spent after nightfall, Sonam seemed pressed, anxious to complete her chores and join the other women and Nordup. They were in the workroom, sorting through the bags of fleeces left by the bursar.

It was difficult to talk above the loud swish as the milk turned; but the silence between us was comfortable. We fell easily into a rhythm of work, counting the number of pulls on the long, slender stem of the whisk, feeling the gradual resistance of the thickening curd, taking turns to rest beside the warm stove. I found myself stealing glances at Sonam, needing to be reassured by the familiar lines and features of her face – its openness, the crinkled, soot encrusted skin, her puckered brow, the half-quizzical look she unconsciously and habitually wore as though she were troubled.

At first I thought her countenance was a consequence of shortsightedness, of her always having to peer through the thick smoke which rose from the stove and lingered in the kitchen air. But I learned to recognize the slightly puzzled, questioning expression at other times and in different circumstances. I realized, too, that she wore it whenever I conjured up her image in my mind's eye.

We finished making the butter and prepared a pot of tea to carry with us to the workroom. From the courtyard we heard the muffled laughter and chatter inside, Nordup's deep voice rising above the rest of the noise. Everyone was there, squashed between the sacks of fleeces and piles of carded wool which lay across the floor. We found a place at the hearth and began work.

Our tasks in the evening with Nordup and the nuns brought an end to the conversations between Sonam and me. I think we were both relieved, and we never spoke of them again.

Twenty-Four

There was no pattern to the weather. The days were rarely the same, but it seemed to me that the changes occurred at night when the sky was secretly transformed. By dawn the nature of the day was already determined. Before I opened the wooden shutters to let in the morning light I often guessed what lay ahead from the different sensations on my skin: the sharp sting of the frosty air on a cloudless day, the dull, numbing cold which came under a grey, snow-filled sky.

We tried to close ourselves off from these daily shifts by spending most of our time inside the winter workroom. Many days were dark; the air was thick and turbulent and light flurries of snow blew through the valley. We braced ourselves; but still the violence of the storm did not return.

There was always movement on the clear, sunny days. People snatched the chance to make journeys before the weather changed and blizzards or bitter desert winds once more confined them to their villages. In the period after the storm we were frequently interrupted in our work by lay visitors resting at Julichang as they crossed the pitted landscape from one place to another. They were offered hospitality by the nuns and we listened avidly to the news they brought from areas made even more remote by the Himalayan winter.

On the cloudless days, too, there was an exodus of monks from Rizong. A number departed for their home villages to pay New Year greetings; others left the monastery to perform household ceremonies in different lay settlements. Often these travelling monks, with bundles of Buddhist texts strapped to their backs, called at Julichang in the early morning. Their excitement was palpable as they sensed again the opening up of the vast terrain before them.

One day, shortly after dawn, the bursar and Rigdol arrived at the nunnery with the medicines I had watched them prepare with the doctor at Rizong. The nuns gathered round eagerly to receive their quota. We were each given four soft yellowish balls to shore up our strength against the rigours of winter (the monks received fifteen each); and Rigdol reminded us to take care to ensure that our supplies lasted until the spring. I followed the example of the nuns who started to nibble at one of the balls. It tasted sweet and sugary. After savouring a morsel, we wrapped the rest in cloth to protect them from the ubiquitous soot and grime, and we stored them with our religious texts on a high shelf above the fire. The distribution of the medicine completed, the bursar hastened to return to the monastery; but Rigdol remained with us, sitting cross-legged beside the hearth until midday. He opened his scriptures and sat quietly reading, occasionally pausing to drink tea or to look up at the nuns working around him. They were pleased – it showed clearly in their faces; and they worked quietly throughout the morning as if it were enough to hear the sound of the paper rustling as Rigdol turned the parchment leaves. His presence restored, at least temporarily, our sense of equilibrium.

Two of the nuns, Samsten and Tsultim, took advantage of the bursar's absence and sought Rigdol's permission to leave the nunnery for several days in order to visit their home villages. Their absence was keenly felt by those of us left behind and their departure seemed to return Julichang to a subdued, almost melancholy atmosphere, which hung heavily over our winter days. The movement of people at this time disrupted our fragile notion of communal stability. Our unease was exacerbated by the absence of Samsten and Tsultim; we missed their distinctive voices and presence at the fireside. No one articulated a feeling of disquiet; but it lurked in the silent pre-occupation of everyone in the workroom.

This prevailing mood sharpened my own feelings of appre-hension, the sense of having lost my bearings as I perceived the crumbling of the order which once underpinned our lives. Often and without obvious reason I was aware of my stomach muscles, tight and knotted. A certain incident, however, gave focus to my general anxiety.

One morning Chuski returned to the nunnery. Her arrival was odd and unexpected. We had been working since day-break in the room off the courtyard with the door closed against the bitter cold, when suddenly the dog's shrill bark alerted us to the arrival of visitors. Tsodpah ran outside to look over the wall, expecting to see monks or lay travellers; but a moment later she was back in the workroom, breathless and excited – Chuski with two Yangthang villagers was approach-ing Julichang. We had not anticipated the return of the pilgrims from their journey round the ancient Buddhist shrines of India and Nepal until the spring. It seemed they had barely departed before they were back; and we puzzled over the early termin-ation of their trip.

We were all peeping through the open door for the first glimpse of Chuski. She entered, smiling shyly. She greeted each of us in a low voice and then, crouching down by the hearth, she slowly stretched her hands over the flames. Chuski was self-conscious; we scrutinized her, looking for signs of change, of familiarity, anxious to know she was still the same Chuski who had departed in the autumn. To her relief, the nuns remembered the villagers hesitating in the doorway. The excitement generated by the party's arrival pushed the awk-ward questions aside and the nuns called out to the men to join everyone else at the fireside.

With little prompting the villagers began to talk about the event of the day before, their flight across the Himalayan peaks from Kashmir; and from time to time Chuski broke in, adding details to the story. The mountain passes had long since closed and the returning pilgrims had waited for days in Srinagar until the skies cleared, before they embarked on their first journey by aeroplane. It was an experience, in the perspective it opened on to the landscape, which left a deep impression on all of them. For the remainder of the day, Chuski spoke of little else other than of what she had seen in the expanse of mountain terrain spread out below her. We listened, waiting for the details to emerge of the rest of her journey. They came but slowly.

The men did not stay long at Julichang. After their departure the noise and commotion in the workroom subsided and we returned to our tasks. Chuski spent the afternoon spinning wool with the other nuns. I watched her deft, slender fingers holding the wooden spindle, pulling and winding the fine thread. After many weeks it seemed strange to see her sitting among us again, yet at times I could believe that she had never been away.

Over the next few days Chuski told the story of her pilgrimage to India. From the outset it had been difficult coping with Chodel's eccentricities; and the party was beset with the problems of negotiating a way through the crowded cities of a foreign country. At all times Chuski was conscious of the teeming mass of people, pressing in, squeezing her space; and each stop the bus made plunged her into a frightening throng of beggars, vendors, roaming animals and stinking, noisy motor vehicles. The pilgrims had travelled by road through Kashmir and into the plains. They reached Dharmsala, their first stop, after a week; and, with some relief, they watched the scenery change once the bus began to climb from the flat, green Punjabi fields into the damp wooded foothills of the Himalayas. Chuski and her companions spent almost two months in Dharmsala, the centre of the Tibetan community in exile. Every day they made a hundred prayer circuits around the Dalai Lama's palace, fervently hoping to catch a glimpse of their spiritual leader. Their patience was eventually rewarded. Early one morning, word passed through the settlement that the Dalai Lama was to give blessings. The visitors from Ladakh joined the long queue of people gathered at the gates of the palace; they shuffled forward, edging nearer to the holy figure, bent low, each clasping a white ceremonial scarf. Two or three hours later, Chuski was blessed. In a low, whispering tone, her face glowing with pride, she described to us how the Dalai Lama had pressed his hand on the crown of her head and presented her with a small ribbon as a symbol of the auspicious moment.

At this point in her story, Chuski paused and, reaching to

the high shelf of the workroom, she took down her bundle of texts. Silently we watched her unwrap the layers of cloth. There, lying among the yellowing parchment pages, we saw the ribbon. The nuns, Dondrup, Nordup and me – we all crowded round excitedly and one by one we were allowed to touch it gently.

On other days Chuski could sometimes be persuaded to talk about the journey into southern India; but her reluctance and discomfort usually forced her to curtail the narrative. Then there was an awkward silence and we pondered over the descriptions of her companion Chodel, her loud, constant chatter, her bizarre behaviour which drew attention to the party. Somehow it all became merged in Chuski's experience with the oppressive chaos of India's urban life and she longed to return to the quiet order of Julichang. We imagined the tiredness, the sickness, the despondency which plagued the travellers as they spent weeks making their way to the Tibetan settlement where Rizong's absentee abbots resided. The pilgrims were granted audiences with the two abbots and they handed over letters and gifts they had carried with them from Memi Nasten and Rigdol. But then the party divided; the monks decided to remain in the south, planning to continue their journey to other Buddhist shrines; the village men, Chuski and Chodel prepared to return to Ladakh. Having arrived in the capital, Chodel remained in Leh.

Although Chuski was quickly absorbed into the routine of nunnery life, there was a residual unease about her return. No one pressed her for more details; rather we turned back to our work, grateful for an extra pair of hands to help with the wool. Now we worked late into the night, carding and spinning until we were barely able to keep our eyes open. Nordup was usually the first to leave; and we would hear him stumbling across the courtyard to the beer room where he slept. Sonam and I followed him outside; the other women simply covered themselves with rough blankets and slept together in the room where we worked.

Alone in the darkness I reflected on Chuski's journey. It struck a discordant note. It seemed ominous that the routine of our small community could have been shattered so easily by an unexpected intrusion from outside.

Twenty-Five

The day I was arrested began like all the others. I cautiously opened my eyes as the pale dawn light seeped through the wooden shutters. I felt the cold stinging my skin and, as it penetrated my consciousness, waking me fully, I remembered that one of the cows was missing. It had strayed from the herd and had vanished into the dark woodland when I returned to Julichang the evening before. Luckily none of the other cows had followed; they had remained together in a docile group, trotting ahead of me along the track to the nunnery.

Dondrup and Nordup went out to look for the missing animal, calling and whistling as they passed along the edge of the trees. But the light had gone and there was no sound on the still night air. They were forced to abandon the search until the following morning.

I lay under the bundle of rags, trying to summon the courage to brave the cold and begin the daily round of chores. I listened for sounds of movement outside, for Nordup's rasping voice; but everything was quiet. My eyes closed again and I dozed. When I next awoke I heard voices on the footpath below the window. I opened the shutters and light flooded in. I knew then it was late and that I must have overslept. As I looked out I could see two nuns heading towards the woodland to resume the search for the stray animal. Quickly I jumped out of bed and hurried to the kitchen. It was deserted; the fire was low and the room was dark and draughty.

I was reluctant to join everyone in the workroom. The day's beginning unsettled me and I felt restless. Awakening for the second time, my mind was full, not of the missing cow but of an incident the day before when I had seen a group of Indian men on the footpath outside Julichang. Instead of walking through the narrow valley from the Leh road, the men had arrived by jeep, driving over the rough stones and covering only the last stretch of the track on foot. They did not come into the nunnery courtyard, but paused to exchange a few words over the wall with Sonam. I peeped through the shutters of the kitchen and observed the interaction. Once the men had continued on their way towards Rizong, I ran down to

Sonam. The men had not spoken Ladakhi and she had found it difficult to understand them. She was puzzled and recounted the exchange to the other nuns. They listened, but barely paused in their work and seemed not to reflect on the strangeness of the episode at all. For me, however, it was full of foreboding.

Later that afternoon the dog warned us of the men's return from the monastery. I left the workroom in case this time they came into the courtyard. I waited in the kitchen until I heard the dog's barking cease and the fading sound of the jeep's engine. I suspected they were looking for me. There was an official air about the party; but no one came into the nunnery and asked directly as to my whereabouts. This puzzled me.

The rest of the day I spent trying to quell my fears: continuing my work with the fleeces, causing laughter among the nuns as I tried to imitate their method of spinning, participating in the chatter around the fire – but my mind was turbulent. Faced with the prospect of expulsion, I experienced once more a surge of powerful feelings. Staying at Julichang now seemed to matter more than anything else. But in casting my mind back over the period since the storm, I knew I had been toying, half consciously, with the idea of departure. Instinctively I had retreated from what I discovered beneath the superficial order of the women's lives. It was another world and I felt I had no place there.

In the late afternoon I set off, as usual, to retrieve the cattle from the mountain slopes. On my way, I called to see the bursar at the monastery. He was sitting on his verandah, taking tea. Rizong was empty; most of the monks were away in the villages and Memi Nasten had gone to Leh to conduct business and to call on Ladakh's chief monks to exchange New Year greetings.

For the first time in many weeks the bursar seemed relaxed and genial. I sat beside him and we talked, passing over events since New Year, discussing visitors to the monastery and nunnery; but he made no reference to the visit of the Indian party earlier in the day. I told him I planned to leave for Leh in the next day or so. I had decided to try and pre-empt what I now anticipated – my arrest. But it came sooner than I thought.

Sonam interrupted my musing on the events of the previous day. She entered the dark kitchen and let out a cry of surprise when she discovered me crouched over the smouldering embers in the base of the stove. I smiled at her, wondering if she had any idea of my inner turmoil; but she said nothing, either about my late appearance or about the missing cow. I was relieved and I watched her moving about the room, humming to herself as she stoked the fire and made preparations for the midday meal. Once the flames were licking the sides of the stove, giving the rough, grimy walls a warm reddish glow, we began to sort quantities of flour.

The reticence between us was eventually broken by Sonam's laughter. She saw my grimace at the prospect of yet another meal of heavy, brown dough and she wrinkled her face in imitation of me. In these winter days there was nothing to break the monotony of our diet, other than a few dried apricots or stale New Year biscuits. Suddenly, as we were working, Sonam remembered that she had put aside some extra supplies of spiced vegetables from the pot prepared months earlier. Eliciting a promise from me that I would tell no one where they were kept, she disappeared into one of the storerooms and emerged with a small bowl of preserves.

At midday I carried the steaming dough across the courtyard to the workroom and Sonam followed with the oiled vegetables. The food was greeted with surprise and delight, and it helped temper the mood of the chilly, subdued morning. Since daylight Nordup and Dondrup had taken turns to comb the woodland and mountains for the stray animal, but it had not been found. Its continuing absence lent weight to our fears that the cow might have wandered down to the river bank and ventured on to the treacherous icy crust which hid the fast-flowing water below.

This lay at the back of our minds as we ate lunch; but afterwards we enjoyed a few moments of distraction and humour as I tried again to master the technique of spinning. My fingers were stiff and clumsy and everyone laughed when the spindle toppled over, almost as soon as I had set it spinning. I gave up and resigned myself to the unskilled work, returning to sort through the bags of greasy, flea infested fleeces stacked in the corner of the room.

Samsten, Tsodpah and Tsultim got to their feet. They were a little unsteady and, after rubbing their cold, cramped limbs, they set off to search for the missing cow in the river valley.

Sonam went out after them into the winter afternoon to collect dried dung and fallen branches for fuel. Often I saw her as I followed the path to Rizong. I would be alerted by the rustle of leaves or the sound of brittle twigs cracking underfoot; then I would catch sight of her moving among the trees. Sonam always looked pensive and absorbed in her own thoughts; and only rarely did she notice me watching her from the path.

After the departure of the nuns, the workroom seemed empty and quiet. Tsering and Damchos crept close to the smoky fire; I worked with Nordup until the yellow light faded from the shaft in the ceiling and the sun had slipped behind the dark valley wall, returning Julichang to shadow. I hurried to leave for Rizong, since I knew there would still be sunshine on the upper slopes of the mountains.

I set off along the track, listening to the creaking noise of the empty wicker basket as it moved about on my back. Before I reached the fork in the path and began my ascent, I heard shouts coming from the woodland. I stopped and looked through the trees. I saw the three nuns climbing up from the river bank, heaving and gasping as they half-carried, half-dragged the missing cow. The animal was in a state of shock, its eyes staring; lumps of ice were stuck to its ragged coat; its body shook in spasms and its legs hung limply down. As I approached the nuns, they explained that they had discovered the cow stranded on the ice and partially submerged in the freezing waters of the river. Their relief at finding it alive showed in their faces; but they dared not linger for fear of its total collapse. They were anxious to return to Julichang where, with Nordup's help, they would try and revive the frightened animal.

I continued on my way, slowly ascending, counting each step and marking my progress by the familiar stones and rocks I passed every day. I felt I knew every curve and incline, every crag and boulder of this dry valley; and often I played games, imbuing certain rocks with magical properties tied to my ability to climb. Once I reached the band of sunshine, I sat down at the side of the path and leaned against a pile of stones. Between the high walls, the air was perfectly still and silent. I heard only the sound of my heart bumping loudly against my chest. I shut my eyes. My stomach muscles were tight and I felt nauseous. For once I could not be soothed by the sun's gentle rays.

A moment later, peeping through heavy, half-closed lids, I saw three men turn the corner. In a second I recognized the green police uniforms and I knew that they had been sent to arrest me. I tried to persuade the men to delay our departure until the next morning: it was late and it would be virtually impossible to reach Leh by evening. They were insistent. They carried orders from the Superintendent of Police and a telegram from the Ministry of Defence in Delhi. I had no alternative but to accompany them down the mountain path to Julichang.

The nuns were gathered at the entrance to Julichang, afraid for me once they had seen the policemen pass the nunnery, heading for the path I had recently climbed. I went to the summer kitchen with Sonam and Chuski and in silence we packed my belongings. Sonam began to cry. I hugged her quickly and, making hurried farewells to the others, I passed out of the nunnery and joined the waiting men. They set off briskly. I could not match their pace and I fell behind; but they turned round at intervals to check that I was still following.

At the edge of the woodland, I paused and looked back. The nuns, Dondrup and Nordup were leaning over the high wall and they waved. Then I lost sight of them. I began the long walk down the dusty track, through the dark valley and into the wide plains beyond.

Index

Achok Rinpoche 44–7
ageing 119–20
alcohol 44, 55, 56–7, 66, 96, 110
altars 7, 47, 51, 82, 83, 88
Ananda (disciple of the Buddha)
    21
anthropology/anthropologists
    19, 24–5, 48, 54, 62
apricots 5, 8, 9, 10, 16, 24, 27,
    54, 55, 84, 108, 120, 137, 151
asceticism 20

barley 27–8, 29, 56
barley flour 6, 18, 25–6, 28, 66,
    67, 81, 123
beer 55, 56–7, 66, 69, 86, 89,
    ♈, 94–7, 103, 108, 109, 110,
    131
begging bowls 22
bodhisattva 76
Bohdgaya 42
Buddha (Prince Gautama
    Siddhartha) 75; becomes
    Buddha 20; seen as a cosmic
    manifestation 76; Doctrine of
    no-self 21; early life 19;
    enunciation of the Middle
    Way 20; Four Noble Truths
    20; and liturgical calendar 43;
    and monasticism 75;
    persuaded to open the order
    to women 21; and pilgrims
    42; reaction to sight of corpse
    19–20; and religious texts
    132; gives teachings & founds
    a community of monks 21;

travels extensively 21; as
    wandering mendicant 20
Buddha (statues) 19, 99, 105
Buddhism, cosmology 79;
    doctrine 45, 46, 134; five
    precepts 44; food
    prohibitions 94; further five
    precepts 44; Hinayana *see*
    Hinayana; introduced to
    Ladakh 23, 76; legends about
    foundation and dissemination
    of 125; long and complex
    history 22; Mahayana *see*
    Mahayana; and marriage 63,
    66; monastic order in ancient
    21–2; and monasticism 75;
    non-violence 33, 89; nun's
    status within 12; place of
    women within 22–3, 41,
    43–4, 47–8, 56; Rizong
    monks and abbots trained in
    Tibet 14; spread of teachings
    63; Tibetan 19, 22, 23, 44–5,
    47, 50, 64, 72, 75–7; wisdom
    76; Yellow Hat school
    consolidates power 24
Burma 75
bursar (Rizong Monastery) 11,
    15–16, 17, 26, 28, 30–35, 43,
    45, 49, 50, 51, 53–7, 59, 63,
    72, 77, 78, 82–7, 90–91, 92,
    95, 98–101, 104, 105, 107,
    108, 117, 118, 122, 123,
    127–9, 134, 137, 142, 143,
    145, 150
butter 7, 8, 11, 16, 17, 77, 78,

81, 85, 103, 123, 143, 144;
"lamps" 7, 50, 51, 88, 94, 99,
105

Cambridge University 19, 24
candles 17, 129
carding wool 41, 57, 120, 121,
127, 144, 148
cattle 1, 7, 11, 15, 16–17, 27,
29, 50, 60, 66, 68, 87, 131,
135–7, 142, 150
celibacy 9, 12, 21, 47, 103
Central Asia 5, 23, 75, 79, 81
Ceylon 75
Changthang 43
charms 65
Chenresig (male deity) 50
China, invasion of Tibet (1959)
24, 79
Chodel 42–3, 147
chomo 12, 13, 28, 29, 30, 32, 33,
48, 55, 56, 58, 59, 70, 72
Chuski 8, 9, 10, 27, 42, 43, 84,
146–8, 153
cloth dyeing 30–32, 86
compassion 76
confession 22
costumes: New Year 106, 110;
wedding 56, 65–6
cremation 19, 79
crows 83, 95, 122

Dalai Lama: and Chenresig 50
office established 24
Dalai Lama, 14th (Tenzin
Gyatso) 14, 22, 42, 79, 147
Damchos 40–41, 49, 109, 119,
120, 135, 152
dancing 44, 106–7
dead, offerings to 89, 101
deaths 19–20, 26, 78–9, 83, 122
Deer Park, Sarnath, near
Benares 20
Defence, Ministry of (Delhi) 2,
153
Dharmsala 22, 23, 41, 42, 45,
64, 78, 79, 134, 147

Dhonden, Yeshe 79
doctor 77–80, 83, 134, 145
Dolma 50, 133
Dondrup 11–12, 16, 17, 56–7,
64, 66, 68, 72, 96, 97, 98, 100,
106, 109, 121, 127, 131, 138,
148, 149, 151, 153
dough 10, 58, 85, 90, 91, 123,
131, 139, 151
dough effigies 7, 51, 52, 60, 88,
89, 92–3, 107, 111
dowry: not required from
novice nuns 21; marriage 56,
63, 66, 69
dye, and animal 'sacrifice' 90
dyeing cloth 30–32, 86

eagles 52
Eight Chief Rules 21
enlightenment 76
evil spirits 65

family life 55–6
fasting 10, 18, 20, 78
femininity 22
Festival of Lanterns 72, 77, 81–5
firewood 57–60, 80
fleas 39–40, 130–31, 151
fleeces 16, 39, 72, 87, 120, 121,
127, 143, 144, 150, 151
footwear 97
forest dwelling 20
Four Noble Truths 20

Gelugpa School 45, 50, 77
Glangdarma, King of Tibet 23
"goat man" 93, 102, 106, 107,
111, 117, 118
goats 7, 17, 88, 89–90, 92–3,
103, 121, 131
goatskins 16, 121
grain 5, 25–9, 55, 87, 92, 117
Greater Vehicle *see* Mahayana

hats 65–6
healers 79
healing rituals 139–40

Hemis Shugba 26, 84, 116, 117
herbs 78, 134
Himalayas 10, 12, 13, 15, 22,
   24, 25, 41, 75, 79, 93, 94,
   124, 126, 134, 135, 138, 140,
   142, 146, 147
Hinayana 75
Hindus 70
hospitality 8, 49, 144
household ceremonies 53–4, 60,
   75, 145

ibex 88, 93
iconography 22
incarnations 14, 45
India/Indians 19; and authorities
   permission to live at
   Julichang 60, 61–2, 68, 70–71,
   97; and author's
   apprehension 2; dye from 31;
   feared by, Ladakhi nuns 43;
   pilgrimage to Buddhist
   shrines in 42, 81, 147; Rizong
   abbots in Tibetan refugee
   settlements in 15, 42; seen
   outside Julichang 149; urban
   life 148
Indus river 14

jewellery 103, 107
Julichang convent 138;
   renowned for apricots 24; and
   authorities' permission to live
   at 60, 61–2, 68, 70–72, 97,
   104; author's life with the
   nuns comes to an abrupt end
   2, 149–53; cattle and goats at
   7; garden 6, 30; integrated
   life at 62, 64; lay visitors 144;
   and New Year 88–90, 93–7;
   lies within a prohibited area
   71; as refuge 9; travelling to
   5, 61, 140–41; visit of
   Rizong's acting abbot 31–2

Kapilavastu 19
karma 20

Kashmir 41, 42, 146, 147
kerosene 17, 53, 61, 95, 99, 129

Lababs 13, 28, 29, 30, 32, 33,
   57, 58
labour tribute 26–7, 54, 55, 89
Ladakh: Buddhism penetrates
   75; and Buddhist food
   prohibitions 94; climate and
   terrain 5, 24; mainly closed
   for security reasons 24;
   dancing in 106–7; ex-Rizong
   abbots make summer visits to
   15; food of 18, 29;
   geographical position 5, 23;
   hats 65–6; hospitality 8; and
   Indian police 61; luxury items
   of 16; Mahayana tradition 75;
   pilgrims in 42, 80, 81; and
   rarity of ordained nuns 12;
   royal household 76; scholars
   establish monastic orders in
   23, 76; songs 139; Tibetans'
   opinion of Ladakhi monks 24;
   trees 57; & Tsering's
   narratives 125; winter in 41
Ladakhi (dialect) 2, 25, 26, 150
Ladakhi New Year 59, 63, 72,
   75, 76, 77, 80, 82–93, 97–111,
   116, 118, 120, 123, 124, 126,
   132, 137, 150, 151
lamas 13, 14, 45
Leh 23, 24, 41, 42, 61, 62, 63,
   69, 70, 71, 86, 87, 104, 139,
   148, 150, 153
Leh road 6, 65, 68, 72, 149
Lesser Vehicle *see* Hinayana
Lhasa 24, 79

Mahapajapati (the Buddha's
   aunt) 21
Mahayana 23, 45, 75, 76
mandala 51
mantras 51, 87
marriage 102
   see also weddings
   arranged 26; dowry 56, 63,

66, 69; and monastery 63;
and polyandry 55
meat 94, 95, 122
medicines 78, 79, 80, 134, 145
meditation 13, 20, 21, 22, 41,
45, 46, 47, 78, 82, 83, 133,
134
Middle Way 20
milk 7, 11, 17, 77, 143
milking 1, 7, 11, 17, 142
monastic cells 7, 15, 77, 78, 116
monasticism 88: and Buddhist
tradition/teachings of the
Buddha 75
monks (main reference)
council of senior 11; nuns
dependent on monks for
ceremonial leadership 22; as
pilgrims 42; power and
authority of 47; rebirth as 64;
and religious texts 44;
training in Tibet 14
motherhood 102
Mungod, India 42
music/musicians 44, 49–52, 65,
66, 102, 103, 106, 107, 110,
117, 118, 139

Namgyal Stonchok, Festival of
15, 43, 47, 48–53, 55, 82
Nasten, Memi 31, 48, 52, 60,
61, 67, 83, 85, 97, 103, 105,
106, 108, 132, 148, 150
Nepal 19, 75
nirvana 20, 64
no-self, Doctrine of 21
Noble Eightfold Path to
salvation 20
non-violence, precept of 33, 89
Nordup 89, 90, 96, 97, 98,
100–103, 106, 108, 121–4,
127, 131, 136, 143, 144, 148,
149, 151, 152, 153
novices 11, 14, 21, 22, 30, 44,
47, 50, 56, 77
Nubra 43
nuns (main references)

acceptance of their lot 41; first
Buddhist 21–2; impressive
range of knowledge of
Julichang nuns 81; lack of
intimacies between 64;
mocked by all sections of
society 23, 43–4; ordained 12;
unremitting physical labour
for the monastery 64; as
pilgrims 42, 81; & rebirth as
a monk 64; and religious
practice 17; weeping of 94–5,
96
Nyima, Tsultim 14, 67

oracles 79
ordination 12, 44, 45

pilgrims 42–3, 49, 80–82, 147,
148
polyandry 55
prayer flags 86–7
prayers 13, 17, 42, 51, 86, 95,
96, 132, 133, 143
printing blocks 87
purification 90

rain retreat 22
rebirth 20, 64, 76, 79
religious festivals 42
religious offerings 7, 31, 47,
53–4, 105, 118, 133, 139–40
religious texts 7, 11, 31, 42, 44,
45, 47, 53, 75, 90, 132, 133,
145, 148
retreat 78
rice, as a fertility symbol 103
Rigdol 45–8, 67, 84, 105, 132,
133, 134, 137, 145, 148
rinpoche 45
Rizong monastery (main
references) abbots of 14, 15,
31–2, 42, 52, 79, 82, 105, 134,
148; altar offerings 7; close
ties with Central Asian
monasteries 79; debating
chamber 134; described 13,

15, 128, 131; economic affairs 11; empire of 11, 26, 48; exodus of monks from 145; and Festival of Lanterns 77, 81–5; goods and labour supplied to 11, 14, 26–7, 28–9, 54, 55, 89, 101; links with Tibetan monasteries 14; and Namgyal Stonchok festival 43, 47, 48–53; and New Year 63, 72, 75, 77, 83, 84, 90–93, 97–108, 116, 123, 132; pilgrims in 49, 81–2; known for its purity and orthodoxy 94; reputation for scholarship, discipline and spiritual integrity 15; storerooms 16, 28, 34, 49, 50, 54, 57, 87, 92, 107–8, 127; temples 13, 15, 48, 49, 50, 51, 52, 54, 75, 82, 83, 84, 90, 98, 99, 100, 101, 102, 103, 104, 105, 106, 109, 117, 118
robes 51, 91, 99, 101, 105, 134; red 2, 9, 97; silk brocade 99; yellow 21
rosary beads 7, 42, 46, 95, 105, 120

"sacrifice" 89, 90
samsara 20
Samsten 27, 28, 31, 43, 49, 66, 69, 109, 116, 117, 118, 121, 125, 126, 127, 145, 151
Saspol 14, 26, 67, 84
scarves, ceremonial 105
scriptures 17, 41, 44, 46, 47, 51, 75, 78, 95, 116, 132, 145
seasons 5, 32–3
sewing 59, 86, 101
Shas (son of Tsultim Nyima) 14
Shas Rinpoche (Rizong abbot) 82
shaven head 9, 12, 21
sheep 89–90, 121, 131
sheepskins 121
shrines 13

skins, animal 121–4
Sonam (cook), 6, 7, 8, 10, 12, 17, 18, 26, 30–35, 39, 40, 42–6, 49, 52, 53, 58, 62, 64, 65, 66, 69, 70, 77, 81, 82, 85, 88, 90, 93, 94, 95, 97, 102, 105, 107, 109, 119, 121, 125, 138–44, 149–53
soul, Buddhist denial of 89
Southeast Asia 75
spinning 41, 57, 72, 120–21, 123, 127, 147, 148, 150, 151
Sri Lanka *see* Ceylon
Srinagar 146
Srinagar-Leh road 71
suffering 20, 63

tanca 13
tea 7–8, 10, 15, 31, 46, 49, 50, 77–8, 81, 91, 92, 105, 107, 109, 132
technology 30
temples: altars 7, 47, 51; cleaning and upkeep 12; lamas in 13
see also under Rizong monastery
Thailand 75
Tibet: Buddhism 19, 22, 23, 44–5, 47, 50, 64, 72, 75, 76, 77; Chinese invasion (1959) 24, 79; Mahayana tradition 75, 76; medicine 79; pantheon of gods and demons 22, 47, 64, 133; proliferation of different schools of Buddhism in 23; Rizong monks and abbots trained in 14; seven auspicious days relating to the history of Buddhism in 43; Yellow Hat school consolidates power 24
Tibetan ("new") calendar 77
Tibetan language 7, 132–3
Tibetan New Year 77
trade routes 23
trading 15, 16, 42, 43, 81

Tsering 40, 41, 46, 49, 109, 120–21, 124–7, 135, 152
Tsodpah 49, 55, 56, 66, 68, 69, 94, 97, 108, 109, 110, 121, 130, 146, 151
Tsongkhapa 24, 50, 72, 77
Tsultim 25–6, 27, 28, 31, 43, 49, 68, 69, 88, 90, 94, 109, 116, 117, 118, 120, 121, 130, 145, 151

Ule Tokpo 32, 33
Urgen 8–9, 11, 34, 85–6, 87, 91–2
Uttar Pradesh 70

Varanasi 42
vegetables 5, 6, 18, 30, 32–5, 50, 52, 63, 67, 84, 87, 98, 104, 107, 123, 151

walnuts 16, 54, 55, 61, 107, 108, 137
washing, body 2, 40, 123
water, fetching 6
weddings 56, 63, 65–9
    see also marriage
wool 57, 72, 120–21, 123, 127, 144, 147, 148

yaks 102, 103
Yangthang/Yangthangers 13, 14, 26, 27, 53–6, 60, 63, 65, 67, 69, 77, 78, 79, 84, 92, 94, 101, 102, 104, 106, 107, 109
Yellow Hat school 24
Yellow Lama 13
yoghurt 17, 29, 30
yogic practice 20

Zanskar 43, 46